# GEORGE ORWELL

Level 4

Retold by Mike Dean
Series Editors: Andy Hopkins and Jocelyn Potter

**Pearson Education Limited**
Edinburgh Gate, Harlow,
Essex CM20 2JE, England
and Associated Companies throughout the world.

ISBN: 978-1-4058-6241-7

First published by Martin Secker & Warburg Ltd 1949
First published by Penguin Books 2003
This edition published 2008

Nineteen Eighty-Four by George Orwell (Copyright © George Orwell, 1949) adapted and simplified
by permission of A M Heath & Co. Ltd. on behalf of Bill Hamilton as the Literary Executor of the
Estate of the Late Sonia Brownell Orwell and
Martin Secker & Warburg Ltd.

5 7 9 10 8 6 4

Text copyright © Penguin Books 2003
Illustrations copyright © Mark Oldroyd (Arena)

Typeset by Graphicraft Ltd, Hong Kong
Set in 11/14pt Bembo
Printed in China
SWTC/04

Published by Pearson Education Ltd in association with
Penguin Books Ltd, both companies being subsidiaries of Pearson Plc

For a complete list of the titles available in the Penguin Readers series please write to your local
Pearson Longman office or to: Penguin Readers Marketing Department, Pearson Education,
Edinburgh Gate, Harlow, Essex CM20 2JE, England.

# *Contents*

# Introduction

*At the end of the hall, a poster covered one wall. It showed an enormous face, more than a metre wide: the face of a handsome man of about forty-five, with a large black moustache. The man's eyes seemed to follow Winston as he moved. Below the face were the words BIG BROTHER IS WATCHING YOU.*

Winston Smith lives in a world where everyone is watched every second of the day. It is a world where Big Brother and the Thought Police control the past as well as the present. They decide what you must do and, even more frighteningly, what you must think.

Winston is secretly unhappy with this life. He seems to be the only person who is dissatisfied with this cruel world. Here, dishonesty and betrayal are rewarded, but truth and love are punished. Alone in his small one-room apartment, Winston keeps a diary of his thoughts and dreams. This is a dangerous activity. If the diary is ever found, Winston will be punished, possibly killed, by the Thought Police. The Thought Police have a *telescreen* in every room in every home and in every public place. They also have hidden microphones and there are spies everywhere . . .

Life is dangerous for Winston, but it would be empty and meaningless without his dreams of a better existence. Will his anger with the Party and his desire for a life outside its control lead him to happiness? Is he alone in his fight against the Party? There must, somewhere, be people like him who also dream of freedom and escape from this terrible life? But even if there were others, how would he know that they were not really working for the Thought Police?

The answer to these questions can all be found in George Orwell's famous but very worrying book *1984*. Written in 1948, when Europe was in a very weak, uncertain condition after the end of World War II, *1984* was an immediate success. Life in Britain at the end of the war was hard, dull and unexciting. Generally, though, people felt proud because they had helped to win an important war and they were still free. They believed that the problems of cruel governments and weak, powerless people belonged to other countries. The Nazis had just lost control of Germany and other European countries, but there were other countries, like Russia and China, where governments seemed to be cruel and the people did not appear to be free. In *1984*, George Orwell skillfully showed readers that dangerous, cruel and powerful governments could happen *anywhere* – even in Britain.

As the real year 1984 came closer, there was an unusual level of discussion about the date, even by people who had not read Orwell's book. If they *had* read the book, they compared the 1984 of Orwell's story with the reality. They did not recognize many similarities. Yes, there *were* more televisions, and we were beginning to see computers in everyday life. But where was Big Brother? Where were the Thought Police? Where were the empty shops, the spies, the boring food and uniforms of Orwell's story? People in many parts of the world were getting richer, not poorer, weren't they? Europeans were becoming more, not less free. A few years later, the Communist governments in Russia and Eastern Europe fell. Surely the world was becoming a safer place, not a more dangerous place? Surely Orwell had been completely wrong?

Nearly sixty years after *1984* was written, though, people are not so sure. In the 'war against terror', many governments are slowly taking more control over people. Cameras everywhere are watching us, and there is information about us all on computers. Big business is destroying the differences between countries, and people are becoming more and more similar in their desires and dreams.

Orwell was not telling us that the world of the future would be exactly the same as the world in *1984*. He was warning us about the possible dangers of power. Winston Smith lives and works in Oceania, where the government is only interested in power. It does not matter to the Party, the people at the top, how they get power and keep it. They do not care about individuals and their feelings, or about happiness, or even about money. For them, the only aim of power is power itself, and they hold power by making people suffer.

'If you want a picture of the future, Winston,' a Party official says to him, 'imagine a boot stamping on a human face – for ever.'

Power can be used to change the reality that we thought we knew. In *1984*, the state has three main ways of doing this. Firstly, it robs people of their natural feelings. Family and romantic love do not exist in Oceania. The society of Oceania demands that people should change their feelings into a love of Big Brother and hate for imagined enemies. During the 'Two Minutes Hate', people shout and scream at pictures of Big Brother's enemy, Goldstein. and a hated Eurasian soldier. Even Winston – who appears to share the Party's beliefs but secretly has his own opinions – cannot stop himself shouting with the rest.

Secondly, the state changes history. In *1984*, Winston Smith's job is to rewrite history. Oceania is always at war with another big country – sometimes Eastasia, sometimes Eurasia. Bombs are always falling, and the people are always frightened. Suddenly, the enemy changes, but the people of Oceania are never told. Instead, history is changed, and they believe that the new enemy has *always* been their enemy. At work, Winston has to change all the old newspapers so no one can ever discover the truth. In this way, the Party can keep control over people's minds. If people never know the truth about the past, how can they ever discover the lies about the present?

A third way of controlling people's minds is through language. One of the central messages in *1984* is the importance of language in human thought. Language shapes and limits our ideas. If the state could control our language, it could also control our thoughts. It would become impossible for people to disobey commands or to have their own ideas. There would be no words with which to think them! In *1984*, a new language, 'Newspeak', is being invented. It will eventually take the place of English and will take away people's ability to think for themselves. In this way, the state will have total control over people's thoughts. Nobody will ever question the Party's power.

Many of Orwell's 'Newspeak' words and ideas have passed into everyday language; for example, *unperson* and *doublethink* (the ability to accept two opposite beliefs at the same time). There are even popular television programmes called 'Big Brother' and 'Room 101'.

The Party believes that Winston, an unbeliever, must be mad. To Winston, the Party is mad. How can anyone say – and believe – that two and two make five? When a man disappears, how can his colleagues say – and believe – that he never existed?

Winston thinks a lot about the reality of his present, and tries to remember the reality of his past. But what is reality? What is truth? Who decides? The individual or the Thought Police? *1984* shows us that there can be no freedom unless ideas and beliefs can be questioned. Without individual freedom, reality belongs to the people with the power. This message is as important to us today as it was when it was first written almost sixty years ago.

George Orwell (whose real name was Eric Blair) was born in India in 1903. After school at Eton, England, he moved to Burma, where he joined the British police for five years. He eventually left because he was unhappy about the British treatment of Burmese people. After doing different jobs in France, he returned to England, where he opened a village shop. Soon, he began writing for magazines. His first book, *Down and Out in Paris and London* (1933), describes his experiences as a poor writer. This book was followed by three works of fiction, *Burmese Days* (1934), *A Clergyman's Daughter* (1935) and *Keep the Aspidistra Flying* (1936). In 1936, Orwell was asked to write about unemployment in the north of England. With his book *The Road to Wigan Pier*, Orwell became one of Britain's most important writers.

In December 1936, Orwell went to Spain to report on the war in Spain. He decided to become a soldier in the government's international army fighting against Franco, and eventually became an officer. In May, 1937, he was shot in the neck. As a result, he was unable to move the left side of his body and he lost his voice for a short time. After leaving Spain, he returned to England and wrote about his war experiences in *Homage to Catalonia* (1938). It was not popular because it criticized British newspapers and politicians for telling lies. It is one of the best books ever written about war, but it sold only 12,000 copies in the first twelve years.

During World War II, Orwell worked for the BBC radio service and for the *Observer* newspaper. He also wrote many articles for magazines, which include some of his best writing.

Orwell's last two books are his most famous. *Animal Farm* (1945) is a story about animals, but it really criticizes the political situation in Russia under a Communist government. Although a lot of his old friends, who admired Russia, hated it, it became one of Britain's most popular books.

Then, in 1948, he wrote his last book, *1984*. The book had a great effect on people's thinking at the time. And, as we have seen, it still makes people think deeply about life, power and society today.

# PART ONE *Thoughtcrime*

## Chapter 1  Big Brother Is Watching You

It was a bright, cold day in April and the clocks were striking thirteen. Winston Smith hurried home to Victory Mansions with his head down to escape the terrible wind. A cloud of dust blew inside with him, and the hall smelled of dust and yesterday's food.

At the end of the hall, a poster covered one wall. It showed an enormous face, more than a metre wide: the face of a handsome man of about forty-five, with a large, black moustache. The man's eyes seemed to follow Winston as he moved. Below the face were the words BIG BROTHER IS WATCHING YOU.

Winston went up the stairs. He did not even try the lift. It rarely worked and at the moment the electricity was switched off during the day to save money for Hate Week. The flat was on the seventh floor and Winston, who was thirty-nine and had a bad knee, went slowly, resting several times on the way. Winston was a small man and looked even smaller in the blue overalls of the Party. His hair was fair and the skin on his face, which used to be pink, was red and rough from cheap soap, old razor blades and the cold of the winter that had just ended.

Inside his flat, a voice was reading out a list of figures for last year's production of iron. The voice came from a metal square, a *telescreen*, in the right-hand wall. Winston turned it down, but there was no way of turning it off completely.

He moved to the window. Outside, the world looked cold. The wind blew dust and bits of paper around in the street and there seemed to be no colour in anything, except in the posters that were everywhere. The face with the black moustache looked down from every corner. There was one on the house opposite. BIG BROTHER IS WATCHING YOU, it said, and the eyes looked into Winston's.

1

Behind him the voice from the *telescreen* was still talking about iron. There was now even more iron in Oceania than the Ninth Three-Year Plan had demanded. The *telescreen* had a microphone, so the Thought Police could listen to Winston at any time of the day or night. They could also watch him through the *telescreen*. Nobody knew how often they actually did that but everybody behaved correctly all the time because the Thought Police *might* be watching and listening.

Winston kept his back to the *telescreen*. It was safer that way – they couldn't see your face. He looked out over London, the biggest city in this part of Oceania. The nineteenth-century houses were all falling down. There were holes in the streets where the bombs had fallen. Had it always been like this? He tried to think back to the time when he was a boy, but he could remember nothing.

He stared at the Ministry of Truth, where he worked. It was an enormous white building, three hundred metres high. You could see the white roof, high above the houses, even a kilometre away. From Winston's flat it was just possible to see the three slogans of the Party written in enormous letters on the side of the building:

WAR IS PEACE
FREEDOM IS SLAVERY
IGNORANCE IS STRENGTH

The Ministry of Truth was called *Minitrue* in Newspeak, the new language of Oceania. *Minitrue*, it was said, had more than three thousand rooms above the ground and a similar number below. The people there worked mainly on news and entertainment. High above the surrounding buildings, Winston could also see the Ministry of Peace, where they worked on war. It was called *Minipax* in Newspeak. And the Ministry of Plenty – *Miniplenty* – which was responsible for the economy. And he could see the Ministry of Love – *Miniluv* – which was responsible for law and order.

The Ministry of Love was the really frightening one. There were no windows in it. Nobody could get anywhere near it unless they had business there. There were guards with guns in black uniforms even in the streets half a kilometre away.

Winston turned round quickly. He smiled. It was a good idea to look happy when you were facing the *telescreen*. He went to his small kitchen. He had not had lunch in the canteen before he left work, but there was no food there except a piece of dark, hard bread for tomorrow's breakfast. He poured himself a cup of colourless, oily gin and drank it down like medicine. It burned him inside, but he felt more cheerful afterwards.

He went back to the living room and sat down at a small table to the left of the *telescreen*. It was the only place in the room where the *telescreen* could not see him. From a drawer in the table he took out a pen and a big diary with beautiful cream paper, which he had bought in an old-fashioned shop in a poor part of the town. Party members like Winston were not allowed to go into ordinary shops, but many of them did. It was the only way to get things like razor blades.

Winston opened the diary. This was not illegal. Nothing was illegal, as there were no laws now. But if the diary was found they would punish him with death or with twenty-five years in a prison camp. He took the pen in his hand, then stopped. He felt sick. It was a decisive act to start writing.

◆

Earlier that morning, a terrible noise from the big *telescreen* at the Ministry of Truth had called all the workers to the centre of the hall for the Two Minutes Hate. The face of Emmanuel Goldstein, Enemy of the People, filled the *telescreen*. It was a thin, clever face, with its white hair and small beard, but there was something unpleasant about it. Goldstein began to speak in his sheep-like voice: criticising the Party, making nasty attacks on Big Brother, demanding peace with Eurasia.

3

In the past (nobody knew exactly when) Goldstein had been almost as important in the Party as Big Brother himself, but then he had worked against the Party. Before he could be punished with death, he had escaped – nobody knew how, exactly. Somewhere he was still alive, and all crimes against the Party came from his teaching.

Behind Goldstein's face on the *telescreen* were thousands of Eurasian soldiers. Oceania was always at war with either Eurasia or Eastasia. That changed, but the hate for Goldstein never did. The Thought Police found his spies every day. They were called 'the Brotherhood', people said, although Winston sometimes asked himself if the Brotherhood really existed. Goldstein had also written a book, a terrible book, a book against the Party. It had no title; it was just known as *the book*.

As Goldstein's face filled the *telescreen* and Eurasian soldiers marched behind him, the Hate grew. People jumped up and down, shouting and screaming so they could not hear Goldstein's voice. Winston was shouting too; it was impossible not to. A girl behind him, with thick, dark hair was screaming 'Pig! Pig!' at Goldstein, and suddenly she picked up a heavy Newspeak dictionary and threw it at the *telescreen*. It hit Goldstein on the nose and fell to the floor.

Winston had often seen this girl at the Ministry but he had never spoken to her. He did not know her name, but he knew she worked in the Fiction Department. He had seen her with tools so he guessed she was a mechanic on the story-writing machines. She was a confident-looking girl of about twenty-seven, and she walked quickly. She wore the narrow red belt of the Young People's League tied tightly round her overalls.

Winston had disliked her from the first moment he saw her. He disliked nearly all women, especially young and pretty ones. The young women were always most loyal to the Party and were happiest to spy on others. But this girl was especially dangerous,

*A girl behind him, with thick, dark hair was screaming 'Pig! Pig!' at Goldstein.*

he thought. Once, when he had seen her in the canteen, she had looked at him in a way that filled him with black terror. He even thought she might be working for the Thought Police. As the screaming at Goldstein increased, Winston's dislike of the girl turned to hate. He hated her because she was young and pretty.

Suddenly he noticed someone else, sitting near the girl, wearing the black overalls of an Inner Party member. O'Brien was a large man with a thick neck and glasses. Although he looked frightening, Winston was interested in him. There was sometimes an intelligence in his face that suggested – perhaps – that he might question the official Party beliefs.

Winston had seen O'Brien about twelve times in almost as many years. Years ago he had dreamed about O'Brien. He was in a dark room and O'Brien had said to him, 'We shall meet in the place where there is no dark.' Winston did not know what that meant, but he was sure it would happen, one day.

The Hate increased. The screaming increased. The voice and face of Goldstein became the voice and face of a real sheep. Then the sheep-face became a Eurasian soldier, walking towards them with his gun, so close that some people shut their eyes for a second and moved back in their seats. But at the same moment the soldier became the face of Big Brother, black-haired, moustached, filling the *telescreen*. Nobody could hear what Big Brother said, but it was enough that he was speaking to them. Then the face of Big Brother disappeared from the *telescreen* and the Party slogans came up instead:

WAR IS PEACE

FREEDOM IS SLAVERY

IGNORANCE IS STRENGTH

Then everybody started shouting 'B-B! B-B!' again and again, slowly, with a long pause between the first B and the second. Of course Winston shouted too – you had to. But there was a second when the look on his face showed what he was thinking. And at that exact moment his eyes met O'Brien's.

O'Brien was pushing his glasses up his nose. But Winston knew – yes he *knew* – that O'Brien was thinking the same thing as he was. 'I am with you,' O'Brien seemed to say to him. 'I hate all this too.' And then the moment of intelligence was gone and O'Brien's face looked like everybody else's.

◆

Winston wrote the date in his diary: *April 4th 1984.* Then he stopped. He did not know definitely that this *was* 1984. He was thirty-nine, he believed – he had been born in 1944 or 1945. But nobody could be sure of dates, not really.

'Who am I writing this diary for?' he asked himself suddenly. For the future, for the unborn. But if the future was like the present, it would not listen to him. And if it was different, his situation would be meaningless.

The *telescreen* was playing marching music. What had he intended to say? Winston stared at the page, then began to write: *Freedom is the freedom to say that two and two make four. If you have that, everything else follows . . .* He stopped. Should he go on? If he wrote more or did not write more, the result would be the same. The Thought Police would get him. Even before he wrote anything, his crime was clear. *Thoughtcrime*, they called it.

It was always at night – the rough hand on your shoulder, the lights in your face. People just disappeared, always during the night. And then your name disappeared, your existence was denied and then forgotten. You were, in Newspeak, *vaporized*.

Suddenly he wanted to scream. He started writing, fast:
*DOWN WITH BIG BROTHER*
*DOWN WITH BIG BROTHER*
*DOWN WITH BIG BROTHER*

There was a knock on the door. Already! He sat as quietly as a mouse, hoping that they would go away. But no, there was another knock. He could not delay – that would be the worst thing he could do. His heart was racing but even now his face, from habit, probably showed nothing.

He got up and walked heavily towards the door.

## Chapter 2  The Spies

As he opened the door, Winston saw that he had left the diary open on the table. *DOWN WITH BIG BROTHER* was written in it, in letters you could almost read across the room.

But everything was all right. A small, sad-looking woman was standing outside.

'Oh, Comrade Smith,' she said, in a dull little voice, 'do you think you could come across and help me with our kitchen sink? The water isn't running away and . . .'

It was Mrs Parsons, his neighbour. She was about thirty but looked much older. Winston followed her into her flat. These repairs happened almost daily. The Victory Mansions flats were old, built in about 1930, and they were falling to pieces. Unless you did the repairs yourself, the Party had to agree to them. It could take two years to get new glass in a window.

'Tom isn't home,' Mrs Parsons explained.

The Parsons' flat was bigger than Winston's and unattractive in a different way. Everything was broken. There were sports clothes and sports equipment all over the floor, and dirty dishes on the table. On the walls were the red flags of the Young People's League and the Spies and a full-sized poster of Big Brother. There was the usual smell of old food, but also the smell of old sweat. In another room someone was singing with the marching music that was still coming from the *telescreen*.

'It's the children,' said Mrs Parsons, looking in fear at the door to the other room. 'They haven't been out today, and of course . . .' She often stopped without finishing her sentences.

In the kitchen, the sink was full of dirty green water.

'Of course if Tom was home . . .' Mrs Parsons started.

Tom Parsons worked with Winston at the Ministry of Truth. He was a fat but active man who was unbelievably stupid and endlessly enthusiastic. He was a follower with no mind of his own – the type that the Party needed even more than they needed the Thought Police.

At thirty-five Tom Parsons had only just been thrown out of the Young People's League, although he had wanted to stay. Before that he had continued in the Spies for a year beyond the official age. At the Ministry he had a job which needed no intelligence, but he worked for the Party every evening, organizing walks and other activities. The smell of his sweat filled every room he was in and stayed there after he had gone.

Winston repaired the sink, taking out the unpleasant knot of hair that was stopping the water running away. He washed his hands and went back to the other room.

'Put your hands up!' shouted a voice.

A big, handsome boy of nine was pointing a toy gun at him. His small sister, about two years younger, pointed a piece of wood. Both were dressed in the blue, grey and red uniforms of the Spies. Winston put his hands up. The look of hate on the boy's face made him feel that it was not quite a game.

'You're a Eurasian spy!' screamed the boy. 'You're a *thoughtcriminal*! I'll shoot you, I'll *vaporize* you!'

Suddenly they were both running round him, shouting 'Spy! *Thoughtcriminal*!' The little girl did everything seconds after her older brother did it. It was frightening, like the games of young, dangerous wild animals that will soon be man-eaters. Winston could see that the boy really wanted to hit or kick him, and was nearly big enough to do so. He was glad that the gun in the boy's hand was only a toy.

'They wanted to see the Eurasian prisoners hang. But I'm too busy to take them and Tom's at . . .'

'We want to see them hang!' shouted the boy, and then the girl started shouting it too.

Some Eurasian prisoners, guilty of war crimes against Oceania, were going to hang slowly in the park that evening. This happened every month or two and was a popular evening's entertainment. Children were often taken to see it.

Winston said goodbye to Mrs Parsons and walked towards the door. He heard a loud noise as a bomb fell. About twenty or thirty of them were falling on London each week. Then he felt a terrible pain in the back of his neck. He turned and saw Mrs Parsons trying to take some sharp stones from her son's hand.

'Goldstein!' screamed the boy.

But Winston was most shocked by the look of helpless terror on Mrs Parsons' grey face.


## Chapter 3  The Ministry of Truth

Winston pulled the *speakwrite* towards him and put on his glasses. To the right of the *speakwrite* there was a small hole, to the left a larger one. In the office wall there was a third hole, larger than the other two.

Messages came to Winston's office through the smallest hole. Newspapers came to him through the middle hole. The largest hole was for waste paper; hot air carried that away. These large holes were called 'memory holes', for some reason.

Today four messages had come through the smallest hole, onto his desk. The messages were about changes to the *Times* newspaper. For example, in Big Brother's speech in the *Times* of

17 March, he had said that South India was safe. The Eurasians would attack North Africa.

This had not happened. The Eurasians had attacked South India, not North Africa. Winston had to re-write part of Big Brother's speech so you could read in the *Times* for 17 March that Big Brother had known about the attack before it happened.

When Winston had finished, his changes to the *Times* went with the newspaper down the middle hole. A new edition would soon appear, with his changes. Every copy of the old edition would disappear. Destroyed. The message to Winston with the changes would disappear down the memory hole, to be burned.

Every day newspapers, magazines, photographs, films, posters and books were all changed. The past was changed. The Party was always right. The Party had always been right. The Records Department, where they destroyed all the old copies of everything, was the largest department in the Ministry of Truth, but there was no truth. The new copies were not true and the old copies had not been true either.

For example, the Ministry of Plenty had said they would make 145 million pairs of boots last year. Sixty-two million pairs were made. Winston changed 145 million to 57 million. So the Party had made five million more boots last year than they expected to. But it was possible that no boots at all were made last year. And it was possible that nobody knew or cared how many boots were made. You could read in the newspapers that five million extra pairs of boots had been made and you could see that half the people in Oceania had no boots.

Winston looked around the office. A woman with fair hair spent all day looking for the names of people who had been *vaporized*. Each of them was, in Newspeak, an *unperson*. She took their names out of every newspaper, book, letter...Her own husband had been *vaporized* last year. She took his name out too.

People disappeared from the newspapers when they were *vaporized* and they could also appear in the newspapers when they did not exist.

Winston remembered Mr Ogilvy. He had appeared in the newspapers because he had led the sort of life the Party wanted. Ogilvy had joined the Spies at the age of six. At eleven he told the Thought Police that his uncle was a criminal. At seventeen he had been an organizer in the Young People's League. At nineteen he had invented a new bomb which had killed thirty-one Eurasians when it was first tried. At twenty-three, Ogilvy had died like a hero, fighting the Eurasians. There were photographs of Ogilvy, but there had been no Ogilvy. Not really. The photographs were made at the Ministry of Truth. Ogilvy was part of a past that never happened.

Anything could be changed. A dreamy man with hairy ears called Ampleforth re-wrote old poems until they supported everything the Party believed in.

But all this work, all these changes, were not the main work of the Ministry of Truth. Most workers in the Ministry were busy writing everything that the people of Oceania read or saw: all the newspapers, films, plays, poems, school books, *telescreen* programmes and songs, the Newspeak dictionaries and children's spelling books.

After his morning's work, Winston went to the canteen. It was full, very noisy and smelled of cheap food and the gin that was sold from a hole in the wall.

'Ah, I was looking for you,' said a voice behind Winston.

It was Syme, his friend from the Dictionary Department. Perhaps 'friend' was not exactly the right word. You did not have friends these days, you had comrades. But some comrades were more interesting than others.

Syme was working on the eleventh edition of the Newspeak Dictionary. He was a small man, even smaller than Winston, with dark hair and large eyes. These eyes were sad but they seemed to laugh at you and to search your face closely when he talked to you.

'Have you got any razor blades?' asked Syme.

'None,' said Winston quickly, perhaps too quickly. 'I've looked for them everywhere.' Everyone was asking for razor blades. There had been none in the Party shops for months. There was always something which the Party could not make enough of. Sometimes it was buttons, sometimes it was wool; now it was razor blades. 'I've been using the same blade for six weeks,' he lied. He actually had two new ones at home.

The people waiting for food and gin moved forward, slowly. Winston and Syme took dirty plates from the pile.

'Did you go to the park yesterday?' asked Syme. 'All the Eurasian prisoners were hanged.'

'I was working,' said Winston. 'I'll see it at the cinema.'

'That's not as good,' said Syme. His eyes looked hard at Winston's face. 'I know you,' they seemed to say. 'I know why you didn't go to see the prisoners die.'

Syme was an enthusiastic supporter of the Party's decisions about war, prisoners, *thoughtcrime*, the deaths in the underground rooms below the Ministry of Love. Winston always tried to move conversation with him away from all that. Syme knew a lot about Newspeak and when he talked about language he was interesting.

'The prisoners kicked when they were hanged,' said Syme. 'I always like that. It spoils it when their legs are tied together. And one of them had his tongue hanging right out of his mouth. It was quite a bright blue. I like that kind of detail.'

'Next, please,' called the *prole* who was giving out the food, and Winston and Syme gave her their plates. She put some grey meat on each one. There was also some bread, a small piece of cheese and a cup of sugarless black coffee.

'There's a table there, under that *telescreen*,' said Syme. 'Let's get a gin and sit there,'

The gin was poured for them into big cups and they walked through the crowded canteen to a metal table. There were some pieces of meat on the table from the last person's meal.

They ate in silence. Winston drank down his gin, which brought tears to his eyes.

'How's the Dictionary?' he said, speaking loudly because of the noise.

'I'm on the adjectives,' said Syme. 'It's wonderful work.' His eyes shone. He pushed his plate away, took his bread in one pale hand and his cheese in the other, and put his mouth near Winston's ear so he did not have to shout. 'The eleventh edition is the final one,' he said. 'We're building a new language. When we've finished, people like you will have to learn to speak again. You think the main job is inventing new words, don't you? Wrong! We're destroying words – lots of them, hundreds of them, every day. We're only leaving the really necessary ones, and they'll stay in use for a long time.'

He ate his bread hungrily. His thin, dark face had come alive and his eyes were shining like the eyes of a man in love. 'It's a beautiful thing to destroy words,' he said. 'For example, a word like "good". If you have "good" in the language, you don't need "bad". You can say "*ungood*".'

Winston smiled. It was safer not to say anything.

Syme continued. 'Do you understand? The aim of Newspeak is to narrow thought. In the end we will make *thoughtcrime* impossible, because people won't have the words to think the crime. By the year 2050 there will be nobody alive who could even understand this conversation.'

'Except . . .' Winston began and then stopped. He wanted to say, 'Except the *proles*.' But he was not sure if the Party would accept the thought.

Syme had guessed what he was going to say. 'The *proles* are not really people,' he said. 'By 2050 – earlier, probably – you won't need a slogan like "freedom is slavery". The word "freedom" won't exist, so the whole idea of freedom won't exist either. The good Party member won't have ideas. If you're a good Party member, you won't need to think.'

One of these days, thought Winston, Syme will be *vaporized*. He is too intelligent. He sees too clearly and speaks too openly. He goes to the Chestnut Tree Café, where the painters and musicians go and where Goldstein himself used to go. The Party does not like people like that. One day he will disappear. It is written in his face.

Syme looked up. 'Here comes Parsons,' he said. You could hear his opinion of Parsons in his voice. He thought Parsons was a fool.

Winston's neighbour from Victory Mansions was coming towards them. He was a fat, middle-sized man with fair hair and an ugly face. He looked like a little boy in a man's clothes. Winston imagined him wearing not his blue Party overalls but the uniform of the Spies.

Parsons shouted 'Hello, hello' happily and sat down at the table. He smelled of sweat. Syme took a piece of paper from his pocket with a list of words on it and studied the words with an ink-pencil between his fingers.

'Look at him, working in the lunch hour!' said Parsons. 'What have you got there, old boy? Something a bit too clever for me, I expect. Smith, old boy, I'll tell you why I'm chasing you. It's the money you forgot to give me.'

'What money?' said Winston, feeling for money in his pocket. About a quarter of your earnings were paid back to the Party in different ways.

'The money for Hate Week. You know I collect the money for Victory Mansions, and we're going to have the best flags around. Two dollars you promised me.'

Winston found two dirty dollar notes and gave them to Parsons. Parsons wrote 'Two dollars' very carefully in small clear letters next to Winston's name in a little notebook. It was clear that he rarely read or wrote.

'Oh, Smith, old boy,' he said. 'I hear that son of mine threw stones at you yesterday. I talked to him about it. He won't do it again, believe me.'

'I think he was angry because he couldn't see the Eurasian prisoners hang,' said Winston.

'Yes! Well, that shows what good children they are, doesn't it? Both of them. They only think about the Spies – and the war, of course. Do you know what my girl did last week? She was on a walk in the country with the Spies and she saw a strange man. She and two other girls followed him and then told the police about him.'

'What did they do that for?' Winston asked, shocked.

'They thought he was a Eurasian spy,' said Parsons. 'They noticed his shoes were different,' he added proudly.

Winston looked at the dirty canteen, looked at all the ugly people in their ugly overalls, ate the terrible food and listened to the *telescreen*. A voice from the Ministry of Plenty was saying that they were all going to get more chocolate – twenty grammes a week. Was he the only one who remembered that last week they got thirty grammes? They were getting *less* chocolate, not more. But Parsons would not remember. And even a clever man like Syme found a way to believe it.

Winston came out of his sad dream. The girl with dark hair, who he remembered from the Two Minutes Hate, was at the next table. She was looking at him, but when he looked back at her she looked away again. Winston was suddenly afraid. Why was she watching him? Was she following him? Perhaps she was not in the Thought Police, but Party members could be even more dangerous as spies. How had he looked when the *telescreen* voice told them about the chocolate? It was dangerous to look disbelieving. There was even a word for it in Newspeak: *facecrime*, it was called.

*Winston ate the terrible food and listened to the telescreen.*

The girl had turned her back to him again. At that moment the *telescreen* told them all to return to work and the three men jumped to their feet.

## Chapter 4 *Ownlife*

Winston sat at the table and opened his diary. He thought of his parents. He was, he thought, about ten or eleven years old when his mother disappeared. She was a tall, silent woman with lovely fair hair. He could not remember his father so well. He was dark and thin and always wore dark clothes. They had both been *vaporized* in the 1950s. His thoughts moved to other women and he started writing in the diary:

*It was three years ago. It was on a dark evening, in a narrow side-street near one of the big railway stations. She had a young face with thick make-up. I liked the make-up. The whiteness and the bright red lips. No woman in the Party wore make-up. There was nobody else in the street and no telescreens. She said two dollars. I . . .*

It was too difficult to continue. Winston wanted to hit his head against the wall, to kick the table over and throw the diary through the window – anything to stop the memory of that night.

It was, of course, illegal to pay a woman for sex. But the punishment was about five years in a work camp, not death. The Party knew it happened. Some *prole* women sold themselves for a bottle of gin and the Party didn't worry much about that. The Party wanted to stop love and pleasure in sex, not sex itself. A request to marry would be refused if a man and a woman found each other attractive. Sex, to the Party, was only necessary to make children.

He thought of Katherine, his wife. Winston had been married. He was probably still married; if his wife was dead, nobody had told him. They had lived together for about fifteen months, nine, ten, eleven years ago. Katherine was a tall, fair-haired girl who moved well. She had an interesting face, until you found out that there was almost nothing behind it. She believed everything the Party said. She had sex only because it was her duty to try and have children. When no children came, they agreed to separate.

Every two or three years since then, Winston had found a *prole* woman who had agreed to have sex for money. But he wanted his own woman. He finished the story in his diary:

*When I saw her in the light she was quite an old woman. She had no teeth at all. But I had sex with her.*

He had written it down at last, but it did not help. He still wanted to shout and scream.

◆

He had walked several kilometres. It was the second time in three weeks that he had missed an evening at the Party Members' Club. This was not a good idea; your attendance at the Club was carefully checked. A Party member had no free time and was never alone except in bed. It was dangerous to do anything alone, even go for a walk. There was a word for it in Newspeak: *ownlife*, it was called, meaning separation from everybody else.

He was walking in a *prole* area near a building that had, in the past, been an important railway station. The houses were small and dirty and reminded him of rat-holes. There were hundreds of people in the streets: pretty young girls, young men chasing the girls, fat old women – the pretty girls in ten years time. Dirty children with no shoes ran through the mud.

The people looked at him strangely. The blue overalls of the Party were an unusual sight in a street like this. It was unwise to be seen in such places, unless you had a definite reason to be there. The Thought Police would stop you if they saw you.

Suddenly everybody was shouting and screaming and running back into their rat-hole houses. A man in a black suit ran past Winston and pointed at the sky.

'Bomb,' he shouted. 'Up there! Bomb!'

Winston threw himself to the ground. The *proles* were usually right when they warned you that a bomb was falling. When he stood up, he was covered with bits of glass from the nearest window. He continued walking. The bomb had destroyed a group of houses two hundred metres up the street and in front of him he saw a human hand, cut off at the wrist. He kicked it to the side of the road and turned right, away from the crowd.

He was in a narrow street with a few dark little shops among the houses. He seemed to know the place. Of course! He was standing outside the shop where he had bought the diary. He was afraid, suddenly. He had been mad to buy the diary, and he had promised himself he would never come near this place again. But he noticed that the shop was still open, although it was nearly twenty-one hours. He would be safer inside than standing there doing nothing outside, so he went in. If anyone asked, he could say he was trying to buy a razor blade.

The owner had just lit a hanging oil lamp which smelled unclean but friendly. He was a small, gentle-looking man of about sixty with a long nose and thick glasses. His hair was almost white but the rest of his face looked surprisingly young. He looked like a writer, or perhaps a musician. His voice was soft and he didn't speak like a *prole*.

'I recognized you when you were outside,' he said immediately. 'You're the gentleman who bought the diary. There's beautiful paper in that diary. No paper like that has been made for – oh, I'd say fifty years.' He looked at Winston over the top of his glasses. 'Is there anything special I can do for you? Or did you just want to look round?'

'I was . . . er . . . passing,' said Winston. 'And I just came in. I don't want to buy anything.'

'Well, that's all right,' said the shop owner, 'because I haven't got much to sell you.' He looked round the shop sadly. 'Don't tell anyone I said so, but it's difficult to get old things these days. And when you can get them nobody wants them.' The old man's shop was full of things, but they were all cheap and dirty and useless. 'There's another room upstairs that you could look at,' he said.

Winston followed the man upstairs. The room was a bedroom with furniture in it. There was a bed under the window, taking nearly a quarter of the room.

'We lived here for thirty years until my wife died,' said the old man sadly. 'I'm selling the furniture, slowly. That's a beautiful bed, but perhaps it would be too big for you?'

Winston thought he could probably rent the room for a few dollars a week, if he dared to. It would be so peaceful to live as people used to live in the past, with no voice talking to you, nobody watching you . . .

'There's no *telescreen*,' he said.

'Ah!' said the old man. 'I never had one. Too expensive.'

There was a picture on the wall. It showed a London church that used to be famous, in the days when churches were famous and people still went to them. Winston did not buy the picture, but he stayed in the room talking to the old man whose name, he discovered, was Charrington.

Even when he left he was still thinking about renting the room. But then, as he stepped into the street, his heart turned to ice. A woman in blue overalls was walking towards him, not ten metres away. It was the girl with dark hair, the one in the Young People's League. The girl must be following him. Even if she was not in the Thought Police, she must be a spy.

The Thought Police would come for him one night. They always came at night and they always caught you. And before they killed you, before you asked them on your knees to forgive you for your *thoughtcrime*, there would be a lot of pain.

## PART TWO  Acts Against the Party

## Chapter 5  A Political Act

Four days later he saw the girl with dark hair again. He was walking to the toilets at the Ministry of Truth and she was coming towards him. She had hurt her hand. She had probably hurt it on one of the story-writing machines – it was a common accident in that department.

The girl was about four metres away when she fell forwards. As she fell, she hit her hand again and cried out in pain. Winston stopped. The girl got to her knees. Her face had turned a milky yellow colour, making her mouth look redder than ever. She looked at him and her face seemed to show more fear than pain.

Winston felt a strange mix of emotions. In front of him was an enemy who was trying to kill him: in front of him, also, was a human being, in pain and perhaps with a broken bone. Already he had started to help her. He felt that her pain was in some strange way his own.

'You're hurt?' he said.

'It's nothing. My arm. It'll be all right in a second.'

He helped her up.

'It's nothing,' she repeated. 'Thanks, Comrade.'

She walked away quickly. Winston was standing in front of a *telescreen*, so he did not show any surprise on his face, although it was difficult not to. As he had helped her up, she had put something in his hand.

It was a piece of paper. He opened it carefully in his hand in the toilet, but did not try to read it. You could be certain the *telescreens* would be watching in the toilets. Back in his office, he put the piece of paper down on his desk among the other papers. A few minutes later he pulled it towards him, with the next job he had to do. On it, in large letters, was written:

*I love you.*

For the rest of the morning it was very difficult to work. At lunchtime in the canteen the fool Parsons, still smelling of sweat, did not stop talking to him about all the work he was doing for Hate Week.

He saw the girl at the other end of the canteen, at a table with two other girls, but she did not look in his direction. In the afternoon he looked at the words *I love you* again and life seemed better. He believed her. He did not think she was in the Thought Police, not now. He wanted to see her again. How? How could he arrange a meeting?

It was a week before he saw her again, in the canteen. He sat at her table and at that moment saw Ampleforth, the dreamy man with hairy ears who re-wrote poems. Ampleforth was walking around with his lunch, looking for a place to sit down. He would certainly sit with Winston if he saw him. Winston had about a minute to arrange something with the girl. He started to eat the watery soup they had been given for lunch.

'What time do you leave work?' he said to the girl.

'Eighteen-thirty.'

'Where can we meet?'

'Victory Square, near the picture of Big Brother.'

'It's full of *telescreens*.'

'It doesn't matter if there's a crowd. But don't come near me until you see me among a lot of people. And don't look at me. Just follow me.'

'What time?'

'Nineteen hours.'

'All right.'

Ampleforth did not see Winston and sat down at another table. Winston and the girl did not speak again and they did not look at each other. The girl finished her lunch quickly and left, while Winston stayed to smoke a cigarette.

◆

He arrived at Victory Square early. Big Brother's picture looked up at the skies where he had beaten the Eurasian aeroplanes (or Eastasian aeroplanes – it had been a few years ago) in the Great Air War.

Five minutes after the time they had arranged, Winston saw the girl near Big Brother's picture, but it was not safe to move closer to her yet; there were not enough people around. But suddenly some Eurasian prisoners were brought out and everyone started running across the park. Winston ran too, next to the girl, lost in the crowd.

'Can you hear me?' she said.

'Yes.'

'Are you working this Sunday afternoon?'

'No.'

'Then listen carefully. Go . . .'

Like a general in the army she told him exactly where to go. A half-hour railway journey; turn left outside the station; two kilometres along the road; a gate; a path across a field. She seemed to have a map inside her head.

'Can you remember all that?' she said, finally.

'Yes. What time?'

'About fifteen hours. You may have to wait. I'll get there by another way.'

She moved away from him. But at the last moment, while the crowd was still around them, her hand touched his – though they did not dare look at each other.

◆

Winston opened the gate and walked along the path across the field. The air was soft and the birds sang.

You were not safer in the country than in London. There were

*Winston saw the girl near Big Brother's picture.*

no *telescreens* of course, but there were microphones and the Thought Police often waited at railway stations. But the girl was clearly experienced, which made him feel braver.

He had no watch but it could not be fifteen hours yet, so he started to pick flowers. A hand fell lightly on his shoulder. He looked up. It was the girl, shaking her head as a warning to stay silent. She walked ahead of him and it was clear to Winston that she had been this way before. He followed, carrying his flowers, feeling that he was not good enough for her.

They were in an open space of grass between tall trees when the girl stopped and turned. 'Here we are,' she said. He stood quite close to her but did not dare move nearer. 'I didn't want to say anything on the path because there might be microphones there. But we're all right here.'

He still was not brave enough to go near her. 'We're all right here?' he repeated stupidly.

'Yes, look at the trees.' They were small and thin. 'There's nothing big enough to hide a microphone in. And I've been here before.'

He had managed to move closer to her now. She stood in front of him with a smile on her face. His flowers had fallen to the ground. He took her hand.

'Until now I didn't even know what colour your eyes were,' he said. They were brown, light brown. 'And now you've seen what I'm really like, can you even look at me?'

'Yes, easily.'

'I'm thirty-nine years old. I've got a wife that I can't get rid of. I've got a bad knee. I've got five false teeth.'

'I don't care,' said the girl.

The next moment she was in his arms on the grass. But the truth was that although he felt proud, he also felt disbelief. He had no physical desire; it was too soon. Her beauty frightened him. Perhaps he was just used to living without women . . .

The girl sat up and pulled a flower out of her hair. 'Don't worry, dear. There's no hurry. Isn't this a wonderful place? I found it when I got lost once on a walk in the country with the Young People's League. If anyone was coming, you could hear them a hundred metres away.'

'What's your name?' asked Winston.

'Julia. I know yours. It's Winston – Winston Smith. Tell me, dear, what did you think of me before I gave you the note?'

He did not even think of lying to her. It was like an offer of love to tell her the truth. 'I hated the sight of you,' he said. 'If you really want to know, I thought you were in the Thought Police.'

The girl laughed, clearly pleased that she had hidden her true feelings so well. She pulled out some chocolate from the pocket of her overalls, broke it in half and gave one of the pieces to Winston. It was very good chocolate.

'Where did you get it?' he asked.

'Oh, there are places,' she said. 'It's easier if you seem to be a good Party member like me. I'm good at games. I was a Group Leader in the Spies. I work three evenings a week for the Young People's League. I spend hours and hours putting up posters all over London. I do anything they want and I always look happy about it. It's the only way to be safe.'

The taste of the excellent chocolate was still in Winston's mouth. 'You are very young,' he said. 'You're ten or fifteen years younger than I am. What did you find attractive in a man like me?'

'It was something in your face. I thought I'd take a chance. I'm good at finding people who don't belong. When I first saw you I knew you were against *them*.'

When Julia said *them* she meant the Party, especially the Inner Party. She spoke about them with real hate, using bad words. Winston did not dislike that. It was part of her personal war against the Party.

He kissed her softly and took her hands in his. 'Have you done this before?'

'Of course. Hundreds of times – well, a lot of times.'

'With Party members?'

'Yes.'

'With members of the Inner Party?'

'Not with those pigs, no. But there are plenty that *would* if they got the chance. They're not as pure as they pretend to be.'

His heart raced. He hoped that the Party was weakened by a lie. 'Listen. The more men you've had, the more I love you. Do you understand that?'

'Yes, perfectly.'

'You like doing this? I don't mean just me. I mean the thing itself?'

'I love it.'

That was what he wanted to hear. The need for sex, not the love of one person, would finish the Party. He pressed her down on the grass. This time there was no difficulty.

Afterwards they fell asleep and slept for about half an hour. Their love, their sex together, had beaten the Party. It was a political act.


## Chapter 6  They Can't Get Inside You


Winston looked round the little room above Mr Charrington's shop. As he had thought, Mr Charrington had been happy to rent it to him. He did not even mind that Winston wanted the room to meet his lover. Everyone, he had said, wanted a place where they could be alone and private occasionally.

They had taken the room because during the month of May they had made love only one more time. ('It's safe to meet anywhere twice,' Julia had said). Then they had had to see each other in the street, in a different place every evening and never for more than half an hour at a time. The idea of having their own hiding place, indoors and near home, had been exciting for both of them.

They were fools, Winston thought again. It was impossible to come here for more than a few weeks without being caught. But he needed her and he felt he deserved her.

Julia was twenty-six years old. She lived in a Party building with thirty other girls ('Always the smell of women! I hate women!' she said) and she worked, as he had guessed, on the story-writing machines. She enjoyed her job, looking after a powerful electric motor. She was 'not clever' and 'did not much enjoy reading' but she liked machinery. Life, as she saw it, was quite simple. You wanted a good time, *they* (meaning the Party) wanted to stop you having it, so you broke the rules as well as you could.

At that moment he heard her on the stairs outside and then she ran into the room. She was carrying a bag. She went down on her knees, took packets of food from the bag and put them on the floor. She had real sugar, real bread, real jam. All the good food that nobody had seen for years. And then ...

'This is the one I'm really proud of. I had to put paper round it because ...'

But she did not have to tell him why she had paper round it. The smell was already filling the room.

'It's coffee,' he said softly. 'Real coffee.'

'It's Inner Party coffee. There's a whole kilo here,' she said.

'How did you get it?'

'There's nothing those Inner Party pigs don't have. But of course waiters and servants steal things, and – look, I got a little packet of tea as well.'

Winston opened the packet. 'It's real tea, not fruit leaves.'

'Yes,' she said. 'But listen, dear. I want you to turn your back on

29

me for three minutes. Go and sit on the other side of the bed. And don't turn round until I tell you.'

Winston looked out of the window. He listened to a woman singing outside with deep feeling. Winston thought she would be quite happy if that June evening never ended. He had never heard a member of the Party sing like that.

'You can turn round now,' said Julia.

He turned round and for a second almost did not recognize her. He thought she had taken her clothes off. But the change in her was more surprising than that. She had painted her face.

He thought the make-up must be from a shop in the *prole* area. Her lips were red, her face was smooth; there was even something under her eyes to make them brighter. It was not well done, but Winston did not know that. He had never before seen a woman in the Party with make-up on. Julia looked prettier and much more like a woman.

He took her in his arms.

'Do you know what I'm going to do next?' she said. 'I'm going to get a real woman's dress from somewhere and wear it instead of these horrible overalls. In this room I'm going to be a woman, not a Party comrade.'

After they made love they fell asleep, and when Winston woke up the hands on the clock showed nearly nine – twenty-one hours. He did not move because Julia was sleeping with her head on his arm. Most of her make-up was on the pillow or on him.

They had never talked about marriage; it was impossible, even if Katherine died. Winston had told Julia about Katherine. She was *goodthinkful*, in Newspeak, unable to think a bad thought. She did not like sex. It was just . . .

'Our duty to the Party.' Julia had said it for him. Just to have children. Children who would one day spy on their parents and tell the Party if they said or did anything wrong. In this way the family had become part of the Thought Police. Katherine had

'You can turn round now,' said Julia.

not told the Thought Police about Winston only because she was too stupid to understand his opinions.

Winston had thought about killing Katherine and once nearly did. But now he and Julia were dead. When you disobeyed the Party you were dead.

Julia woke up and put her hands over her eyes.

'We are the dead,' Winston said.

'We're not dead yet,' said Julia, pressing her body against his.

'We may be together for another six months – a year. When they find us there will be nothing either of us can do for the other.'

'We will tell them everything,' she said. 'Everybody always does. They make you feel so much pain.'

'Even if we tell them everything, that's not a betrayal. The betrayal would only be if they made me stop loving you.'

She thought about that. 'They can't do that,' she said finally. 'It's the one thing they can't do. They can make you say anything – *anything* – but they can't make you believe it. They can't get inside you.'

'No,' he said, a little more hopefully. 'No, that's quite true. They can't get inside you.'

'I'll get up and make some coffee,' she said. 'We've got an hour. What time do they turn the lights off at your flats?'

'Twenty-three thirty.'

'It's twenty-three hours at the Party building. But you have to get in earlier than that because . . .'

She suddenly reached down from the bed to the floor, picked up a shoe and threw it hard into the corner of the room.

'What was it?' he said in surprise.

'A rat. I saw his horrible little nose. There's a hole down there. I frightened him, I think.'

'Rats!' said Winston quietly. 'In this room!'

'They're everywhere,' said Julia, without much interest, as she lay down again. 'We've even got them in the kitchen at the Party building. Did you know they attack children? In some parts of London a woman daren't leave a baby alone for two minutes. The big brown ones are the worst. They . . .'

'*Stop! Stop!*' said Winston, his eyes tightly shut.

'Dearest! You've gone quite pale. What's the matter?'

'They are the most horrible things in the world – rats!'

She put her arms round him but he did not re-open his eyes immediately.

'I'm sorry,' he said. 'It's nothing. I don't like rats, that's all.'

'Don't worry, dear. We won't have the dirty animals in here. I'll put something over the hole before we go.'

Julia got out of bed, put on her overalls and made the coffee. The smell was so powerful and exciting that they shut the window, worried that somebody outside would notice it and ask questions. And they could taste the real sugar in the coffee – it was even better than the taste of the coffee itself.

Julia walked round the room with one hand in her pocket and a piece of bread and jam in the other. She looked at the books without interest. She told Winston the best way to repair the table. She sat down in the old armchair to see if it was comfortable. She smiled at the old twelve-hour clock.

'How old is that picture over there, do you think?' she asked. 'A hundred years old?'

'More. Two hundred. But it's impossible to discover the age of anything these days.'

She looked at it. 'What is this place?'

'It's a church. Well, that's what it used to be.'

When Winston got out of bed it was dark. The room was a world, a past world, and they were the last two people from it who were still living.

# Chapter 7  Our Leader, Emmanuel Goldstein

They *vaporized* Syme. One morning he was not at work; a few careless people talked about his absence. On the next day nobody talked about him. His name disappeared from lists and newspapers. He did not exist. He had never existed.

Parsons was helping to organize Hate Week. He was completely happy, running around painting posters, singing the new Hate Song, smelling even more strongly of sweat in the hot weather.

Daily life no longer caused Winston pain: He had stopped drinking gin at all hours and his knee felt better. He did not want to shout angry words at the *telescreen* all the time.

He met Julia four, five, six – seven times during the month of June. It was so hot at the end of the month that they lay on the bed in the room over Mr Charrington's shop without clothes on. The rat had never come back.

Sometimes they talked about a more open war against the Party, but they did not know how to begin. Winston told her about the strange understanding that seemed to exist between himself and O'Brien. He sometimes felt like going to see him, telling him he was the enemy of the Party, demanding O'Brien's help. Strangely, Julia did not think this was a wild idea. She judged people by their faces and it seemed natural to her that the look in O'Brien's eyes made Winston believe in him. Also, she thought that everybody secretly hated the Party, although she did not believe in Goldstein and the Brotherhood; she thought the Party had invented them.

And then at last it happened. All his life, it seemed to him, he had been waiting for this: there was a message from O'Brien.

◆

Winston was outside his office at the Ministry when he heard a small cough behind him and turned. It was O'Brien.

'I was reading your Newspeak article the other day. You know a lot about Newspeak, I believe.'

'Oh, not really. I've never invented any of the words . . .'

'But you write it very well,' said O'Brien. 'That is not only my own opinion. I was talking recently to a friend of yours who knows a lot about Newspeak. I can't remember his name at the moment.'

Winston's heart jumped. This could only mean Syme. But Syme was not only dead, he was *vaporized*, an *unperson*. It was dangerous to talk about an *unperson*; they could kill you for it. O'Brien was sharing a *thoughtcrime* with him.

'In your Newspeak article you used two words which we have recently taken out of the language,' said O'Brien. 'Have you seen the new tenth edition?'

'No,' said Winston. 'We still have the ninth in the office.'

'The tenth will not be sent to offices for some months, but I have one. Would you like to see it, perhaps?'

'Yes, very much,' said Winston, who could see where this was leading.

'You will be interested, I'm sure. You will like the smaller number of verbs. Shall I send someone to you with the Dictionary? But I always forget that kind of thing. Perhaps you could collect it from my flat at a convenient time? Wait. Let me give you my address.'

They were standing in front of a *telescreen* which could see what he was writing. He wrote an address in a notebook, pulled out the page and gave it to Winston.

'I am usually at home in the evenings,' he said. 'If not, my servant will give you the Dictionary.'

And then he was gone.

◆

They had done it, they had done it at last!

The room was long, carpeted and softly lit; the sound from the *telescreen* was low. At the far end of the room O'Brien was sitting under a lamp with papers on either side of him. He did not look up when the servant showed Winston and Julia in.

Winston's heart was beating fast. It was dangerous to arrive with Julia, although they had met only outside O'Brien's flat. And although O'Brien had invited him, he was still afraid of the black-uniformed guards in this enormous building with its strange smells of good food and tobacco. But the guards had not ordered him out.

O'Brien continued to work and did not look pleased at the visit. It seemed quite possible to Winston that he had just made a stupid mistake. He could not even pretend that he had come only to borrow the Dictionary – if he had, why was Julia here?

O'Brien got up slowly from his chair and came towards them across the thick carpet. He pressed a switch on the wall and the voice from the *telescreen* stopped.

Julia gave a small cry of surprise and without thinking Winston said, 'You can turn it off!'

'Yes,' said O'Brien. 'We can turn it off. We in the Inner Party are allowed to do that.'

Nobody spoke. Without the voice from the *telescreen* the room was completely silent. Then O'Brien smiled.

'Shall I say it or will you?' he said.

'*I* will say it,' said Winston immediately. 'That thing is really turned off?'

'Yes. We are alone.'

Winston paused. He did not know exactly what he expected from O'Brien. Then he continued, 'We believe that there is a secret organization working against the Party and that you are part of it. We want to join it and work for it. We are enemies of the Party. We are lovers, and we are *thoughtcriminals*. And now we are in your power.'

'We are enemies of the Party.'

O'Brien took a bottle and filled three glasses with dark red liquid. It reminded Winston of something he had seen a long time ago. Julia picked up her glass and smelled the liquid with great interest.

'It is called wine,' said O'Brien with a small smile. 'Not much of it gets to ordinary Party members, I'm afraid.' His face became serious again, and he lifted his glass: 'To our Leader,' he said. 'To Emmanuel Goldstein.'

Winston lifted his glass, wide-eyed. Wine was a thing he had read and dreamed about. For some reason he always thought it tasted sweet. But it tasted of nothing. The truth was that after years of drinking gin he could taste almost nothing.

'So Goldstein is a real person?' he said.

'Yes he is, and he is alive. Where, I do not know.'

'And the Brotherhood is real, too? It was not invented by the Thought Police?'

'No, it is real. But you will never learn much more about the Brotherhood than that.' He looked at his watch. 'It is unwise even for me to turn the *telescreen* off for more than half an hour. It was a mistake for both of you to arrive here together, and you, Comrade,' – he looked at Julia – 'will have to leave first. We have about twenty minutes. Now, what are you prepared to do?'

'Anything that we can,' said Winston.

O'Brien had turned himself a little in his chair so that he was looking at Winston. He seemed to think that Winston could answer for Julia.

'You are willing to give your lives?'

'Yes.'

'You are willing to murder another person?'

'Yes.'

'You are willing to cause the death of hundreds of innocent people?'

'Yes.'

'If, for example, it would help us to blind a child and destroy its face – would you do that?'

'Yes.'

'Are you willing to kill yourselves, if we order you to do so?'

'Yes.'

'You are willing, the two of you, to separate and never see each other again?'

'No!' shouted Julia.

It seemed to Winston that a long time passed before he answered. 'No,' he said finally.

'You did well to tell me,' said O'Brien. 'It is necessary for us to know everything.'

O'Brien started walking up and down, one hand in the pocket of his black overalls, the other holding a cigarette.

'You understand,' he said, 'that secrets will always be kept from you. You will receive orders and you will obey them without knowing why. Later I shall send you a book by Emmanuel Goldstein. When you have read the book you will be full members of the Brotherhood. When you are finally caught you will get no help. Sometimes we are able to get a razor blade into the prison to silence someone, but you are more likely to tell them all you know – although you will not know very much. We are the dead. We are fighting for a better life for people in the future.' He stopped and looked at his watch. 'It is almost time for you to leave, Comrade,' he said to Julia. 'Wait. There is still some wine.' He filled the glasses and held up his own glass. 'What shall we drink to? To the death of Big Brother? To the future?'

'To the past,' said Winston.

'Yes, the past is more important,' said O'Brien seriously.

They finished the wine and a moment later Julia stood up to go. When she had left, Winston stood up and he and O'Brien shook hands. At the door he looked back, but O'Brien was already at his desk, doing his important work for the Party.

# Chapter 8  *Doublethink*

On the sixth day of Hate Week, just before two thousand Eurasian prisoners were hanged in the park, the people of Oceania were told that they were not at war with Eurasia now. They were at war with Eastasia and Eurasia was a friend. You could hear it on the *telescreens* – Oceania was at war with Eastasia: Oceania had always been at war with Eastasia.

Winston had worked more than ninety hours in the last five days of Hate Week. Now he had finished and he had nothing to do, no Party work until tomorrow morning. Slowly, in the afternoon sunshine, he walked up a narrow street to Mr Charrington's shop, watching for the Thought Police, but sure – although he had no reason to be sure – that he was safe. In his case, heavy against his legs, he carried *the book*, Goldstein's book. He had had it for six days but had not looked at it yet.

Tired but not sleepy, he climbed the stairs above Mr Charrington's shop. He opened the window and put the water on for coffee. Julia would be here soon. He took Goldstein's book out of his case and opened it. Then he heard Julia coming up the stairs and jumped out of his chair to meet her. She put her brown tool bag on the floor and threw herself into his arms. It was more than a week since they had seen each other.

'I've got *the book*,' he said.

'Oh, you've got it? Good,' she said without much interest, and almost immediately bent down to make the coffee.

They did not talk about the book again until they had been in bed for half an hour. It was evening and just cool enough to have a blanket over them. Julia was falling asleep by his side. Winston picked the book up from the floor and sat up in bed.

'We must read it,' he said. 'You too. All members of the Brotherhood have to read it.'

'You read it,' she said with her eyes shut. 'Read it to me, that's the best way. Then you can explain it to me.'

The clock's hands said six, meaning eighteen. They had three or four hours ahead of them. He put the book against his knee and began reading:

*There have always been three kinds of people in the world, the High, the Middle and the Low. The world has changed but society always contains these three groups.*

'Julia, are you awake?' said Winston.

'Yes, my love, I'm listening.'

*The aims of the three groups are completely different. The High want to stay where they are. The Middle want to change places with the High. Sometimes the Low have no aim at all, because they are too tired from endless boring work to have an aim. If they do have one, they want to live in a new world where all people are equal.*

*At the beginning of the twentieth century this equality became possible for the first time because machines did so much of the work. A centuries-old dream seemed to be coming true. But in the early 1930s the High group saw the danger to them of equality for all and did everything possible to stop it.*

*The individual suffered in ways that he had not suffered for centuries. Prisoners of war were sent into slavery or hanged. Thousands were sent to prison although they had broken no law. The populations of whole countries were forced to leave their homes. And all this was defended and even supported by people who said they believed in progress.*

*The people who entered the new High group were from the professions: scientists, teachers, journalists. They used newspapers, radio, film and television to control people's thoughts. When a television that could both send and receive information was invented, private life came to an end. Every individual, or at least every important individual, could be watched twenty-four hours a day. For the first time it was possible to force people to obey the Party and to share the Party's opinion on all subjects.*

*After the 1950s and 1960s the danger of equality had been ended and society had re-grouped itself, as always, into High, Middle and Low.*

41

*But the new High group, for the first time, knew how to stay in that position for ever.*

*First, in the middle years of the twentieth century, the Party made sure that it owned all the property – all the factories, land, houses, everything except really small pieces of personal property. This meant that a few people (the Inner Party) owned almost everything and the Middle and Low groups owned nearly nothing. There was therefore no hope of moving up in society by becoming richer and owning more.*

*But the problem of staying in power is more complicated than that. In the past, High groups have fallen from power either because they have lost control of the Middle or Low groups or because they have become too weak, or because they have been attacked and beaten by an army from outside.*

*After the middle of the century there was really no more danger from the Middle or Low groups. The Party had made itself stronger by killing all of its first leaders (people like Jones, Aaronson and Rutherford). By 1970 Big Brother was the only leader and Emmanuel Goldstein was in hiding somewhere.*

*The Party then kept itself strong. The child of Inner Party parents is not born into the Inner Party; there is an examination, taken at the age of sixteen. Weak Inner Party members are moved down and clever Outer Party members are allowed to move up. Although proles do not usually move up into the Party, the Party always stops itself from becoming stupid or weak.*

*The Party has also made attack from the outside impossible. There are now only three great countries in the world. They are always at war but none of them can win or even wishes to win these wars. Following the idea of 'doublethink' the mind of the Party, which controls us all, both knows and does not know the aim of these wars. The aim is to use everything that a country produces without making its people richer. If people became richer, there would be an end to the world of the High, the Middle and the Low. The Low and the Middle would not wish to stay in their places and would not need to.*

The Middle and Low are kept in their places by their belief in the wars that none of the three countries can win. So the Party has to end independent thought and make people believe everything they are told. The Party must know what every person is thinking, so they never want to end the war. War continues, always and for ever.

People are given somewhere to live, something to wear and something to eat. That is all they need and they must never want more. They are given work, but only the Thought Police do their work really well.

All good things in the world of Oceania today, all knowledge, all happiness, come from Big Brother. Nobody has ever seen Big Brother. He is a face on posters, a voice on the telescreen. We can be sure that he will never die. Big Brother is the way the Party shows itself to the people.

Below Big Brother comes the Inner Party, which is now six million people, less than 2% of the population of Oceania. Below the Inner Party comes the Outer Party. The Inner Party is like the mind of the Party and the Outer Party is like its hands. Below that come the millions of people we call 'the proles', about 85% of the population.

A Party member lives under the eye of the Thought Police from birth to death. Even when he is alone he can never be sure he is alone. He will never make a free choice in his life.

But there is no law and there are no rules. They are not necessary. Most people know what they must do – in Newspeak they are 'goodthinkers'. And since Party members were children they have been trained in three more Newspeak words: 'crimestop', 'blackwhite' and 'doublethink'.

Even young children are taught 'crimestop'. It means stopping before you think a wrong thought. When you are trained in 'crimestop' you cannot think a thought against the Party. You think only what the Party wants you to think.

But the Party wants people to think different thoughts all the time. The important word here is 'blackwhite.' Like many Newspeak words, this has two meanings. Enemies say that black is white – they tell lies. But Party members say that black is white because the Party tells them to *and because they believe it. They must forget that they ever had a different belief.*

*'Blackwhite' and 'crimestop' are both part of 'doublethink'. 'Doublethink' allows people to hold two different ideas in their minds at the same time – and to accept both of them. In this way they can live with a changing reality, including a changing past. The past must be changed all the time because the Party can never make a mistake. That is the most important reason. It is also important that nobody can remember a time better than now and so become unhappy with the present. By using 'doublethink' the Party has been able to stop history, keep power and . . .*

'Julia?'

No answer.

'Julia, are you awake?'

No answer. She was asleep. He shut the book, put it carefully on the floor, lay down and put the blanket over both of them. The book had not told him anything he did not already know, but after reading it he knew he was not mad. He shut his eyes. He was safe, everything was all right.

When he woke he thought he had slept a long time but, looking at the old clock, he saw it was only twenty-thirty. Outside he could hear singing. It was a song written in the Ministry of Truth and a *prole* woman was singing it. If there was hope, thought Winston, it was because of the *proles*. Even without reading the end of Goldstein's book, he knew that was his message. The future belonged to the *proles*; Party members were the dead.

'We are the dead,' he said.

'We are the dead,' agreed Julia.

'You are the dead,' said a voice behind them.

They jumped away from each other. Winston felt his blood go cold. Julia's face had turned a milky yellow.

'You are the dead,' repeated the voice.

'It was behind the picture,' breathed Julia.

'It was behind the picture,' said the voice. 'Stay exactly where you are. Do not move until we order you to.'

It was starting, it was starting at last! They could do nothing except look into each other's eyes. They did not even think of running for their lives or getting out of the house before it was too late. It was unthinkable to disobey the voice from the wall.

There was a crash of breaking glass. The picture had fallen to the floor. There was a *telescreen* behind it.

'Now they can see us,' said Julia.

'Now we can see you,' said the voice. 'Stand in the middle of the room. Stand back to back. Put your hands behind your heads. Do not touch each other.'

'I suppose we should say goodbye,' said Julia.

'You should say goodbye,' said the voice.

There was a crash as a ladder broke through the window. Soldiers came in; more came crashing in through the door.

Winston did not move, not even his eyes. Only one thing mattered: don't give them an excuse to hit you.

One of the soldiers hit Julia hard in the stomach. She fell to the floor, fighting to breathe. Then two of them picked her up and carried her out of the room, holding her by the knees and shoulders. Winston saw her face, yellow with pain, with her eyes tightly shut as they took her away from him.

He did not move. No one had hit him yet. He wondered if they had got Mr Charrington. He wanted to go to the toilet. The clock said nine, meaning twenty-one hours, but the light seemed too strong for evening. Was it really nine in the morning? Had he and Julia slept all that time?

Mr Charrington came into the room and Winston suddenly realized whose voice he had heard on the *telescreen*. Mr Charrington still had his old jacket on, but his hair, which had been almost white, was now black. His body was straighter and

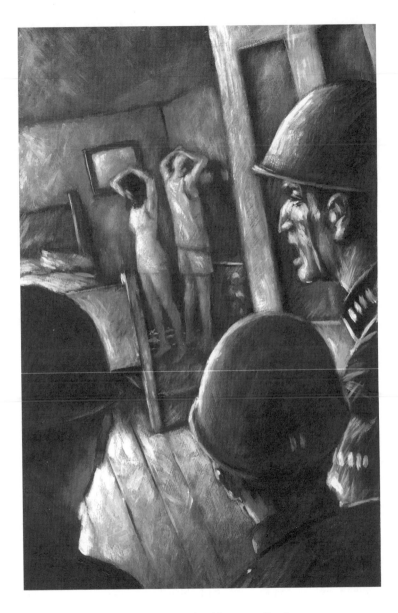

'I suppose we should say goodbye.'

looked bigger. His face was the clear-thinking, cold face of a man of about thirty-five. Winston realized that for the first time in his life he was looking at a member of the Thought Police.

## PART THREE  Inside Winston Smith's Head

### Chapter 9  *Miniluv*

He did not know where he was. He thought he was in the Ministry of Love, *Miniluv*, but he could not be certain.

He was in a high-ceilinged, windowless cell with white stone walls. It was bright with cold light. In this place, he felt, the lights would never be turned out. One moment he felt certain that it was bright day outside and the next moment he was equally certain that it was black night. 'We shall meet in the place where there is no dark,' O'Brien had said to him. In the Ministry of Love there were no windows.

He thought of O'Brien more often than Julia. He loved Julia and would not betray her, but he did not think about what was happening to her. Sometimes he thought about what they would do to him. He saw himself on the floor, screaming through broken teeth for them to stop hitting him. O'Brien must know he was here. O'Brien said the Brotherhood never tried to save its members. But they would send him a razor blade if they could. One cut and it would all be finished.

In his cell, there was a continuous noise from the machine that brought air in from outside. A narrow shelf went round the wall, stopping only at the door, and at the end opposite the door there was a toilet with no wooden seat. There were four *telescreens*, one in each wall.

He was hungry. It might be twenty-four hours since he had eaten, it might be thirty-six. He still did not know, probably never would know, if it had been morning or evening when the soldiers took him. Since then he had been given no food.

He sat on the narrow shelf without moving, with his hands crossed on his knees. He had already learned not to move too much. If you moved around they shouted at you from the *telescreen*. But he wanted food so badly, especially a piece of bread. He thought perhaps there was a small piece in the pocket of his overalls. His need for the bread grew stronger than the fear; he put a hand in his pocket.

'Smith!' shouted a voice from the *telescreen*. '6079 Smith W! Hands out of pockets in the cells!'

He crossed his hands on his knee again. There was a sound of marching boots outside. A young officer, black-uniformed, with an emotionless face, stepped into the cell. He waved to the guards behind him and they brought in a man who they were holding by the arms. It was Ampleforth, the man who re-wrote poems for the Party. The cell door closed behind him.

Ampleforth walked up and down the cell. He had not yet noticed Winston. He was dirty, wore no shoes and had not shaved for several days. The hairy half-beard gave him a criminal look that was strange, with his large weak body and nervous movements.

Winston thought quickly. He must speak to Ampleforth even if they shouted at him through the *telescreen*. It was possible that Ampleforth had the razor blade for him.

'Ampleforth,' he said.

There was no shout from the *telescreen*. Ampleforth stopped walking up and down. He seemed surprised. It took him a moment to recognize Winston.

'Ah, Smith!' he said. 'You too!'

'What are you in for?'

Ampleforth put a hand to his head, trying to remember. 'There is something . . .' he said. 'We were working on a poem and I didn't change the word "God". It was necessary, in the poem. There was no other word. So I left it.' For a moment he looked happy, pleased with his work on the poem.

'Do you know what time of day it is?' asked Winston.

Ampleforth looked surprised. 'I hadn't thought about it. They took me – it could be two days ago – perhaps three.' He looked round the cell. 'There is no difference between night and day in this place. You can never know the time.'

They talked for a few minutes, then, for no clear reason, a voice from the *telescreen* told them to be silent. Winston sat quietly, his hands crossed. Ampleforth was too large for the narrow shelf and moved from side to side. Time passed – twenty minutes, an hour. Again there was a sound of boots. Winston's stomach turned to water. Soon, very soon, perhaps now, the boots would come for him.

The door opened. The cold-faced young officer stepped into the cell. He waved his arm at Ampleforth.

'Room 101,' he said.

Ampleforth marched out between the guards. He looked a little worried but did not seem to understand what was happening to him.

More time passed. It seemed like a long time to Winston. He had only six thoughts: the pain in his stomach; a piece of bread; the blood and the screaming; O'Brien; Julia; the razor blade.

Then his stomach turned to water again as he heard the boots outside. The door was opened and a smell of sweat came in with the cold air. Parsons walked into the cell.

'*You* here!' Winston cried out in surprise.

Parsons did not seem interested in Winston or surprised to see him. He looked completely without hope.

'What are you in for?' said Winston.

'*Thoughtcrime*,' said Parsons, almost crying. 'They won't shoot me, will they? I mean, they don't shoot you when you haven't done anything – just thought? And they'll know everything I've done for the Party, won't they? I'll just get five years, don't you think? Or even ten years? Someone like me could really help the Party in prison. They wouldn't shoot me for just one mistake?'

'Are you guilty?' said Winston.

'Of course I'm guilty!' said Parsons, looking at the *telescreen* as he spoke. 'I wouldn't be here if I wasn't. *Thoughtcrime* is a terrible thing. Do you know how it happened? In my sleep! Yes, there I was working away for the Party – I never knew I had any bad stuff in my mind at all. And then I started talking in my sleep. Do you know what I said? I said "Down with Big Brother!" Do you know what I'm going to say to them? I'm going to say, "Thank you for saving me." '

'Who told them about you?' said Winston.

'My little daughter,' said Parsons, sad but proud. He walked up and down a few more times, looking hard at the toilet. 'Excuse me, old man,' he said. 'I can't help it. It's the waiting.'

Parsons took his trousers down. Winston covered his face with his hands.

'Smith!' shouted the voice from the *telescreen*. '6079 Smith W! Uncover your face. No faces covered in the cells.'

Winston uncovered his face. Parsons used the toilet, loudly and horribly. The cell smelled terrible for hours afterwards.

Parsons was taken out. More men and women were brought in and taken out again by the guards. One woman was sent to 'Room 101' and seemed to become smaller and change colour as she heard the words.

'Comrade! Officer!' she cried. 'You don't have to take me to that place! Haven't I told you everything already? I'll say anything. Just write it down and I'll say it! Not Room 101.'

'Room 101,' said the guard.

A long time passed. Winston was alone and had been alone for hours. Sometimes he thought of O'Brien and the razor blade, but with less and less hope. He also thought, less clearly, of Julia. He thought that if she were in pain and he could double his own pain to help her, he would do it.

He heard the boots again. O'Brien came in. Winston got to his feet. The shock made him forget the *telescreen* for the first time in years.

'They've got you too!' he shouted out.

'They got me a long time ago,' said O'Brien with a small smile. He stepped to one side. Behind him there was a large guard with a heavy stick in his hand.

'You knew this, Winston,' said O'Brien. 'You have always known it.'

Yes, he had always known it. But there was no time to think of that. The heavy stick in the guard's hand might hit him anywhere, on his head, ear, arm, elbow . . .

The elbow! He had gone down on his knees, holding the pain in his elbow with the other hand. There was an explosion of yellow light. The pain was unbelievable, but the guard had only hit him once. They were both looking down at him and the guard was laughing.

Well, one question was answered. You could never, for any reason on earth, wish for more pain. You only wished for one thing – that it would stop. Nothing in the world was as bad as physical pain. With pain there are no heroes, no heroes, he thought again and again as he lay screaming on the floor, holding his useless left arm.

## Chapter 10  Two and Two Make Five

He was lying on a bed and he could not move. There was a strong light in his face. The damage to his elbow had only been the start of it. Five or six men in black uniforms had hit him with sticks or iron bars, kicked him with their boots . . .

He could not remember how many times they had hit him or how long this punishment had lasted. Sometimes he told them what they wanted to know before they even touched him. Other times they hit him again and again before he said a word. And all this was just the start – the first stage of questioning that everyone in the cells of the Ministry of Love had to suffer.

Later the questioners were not guards but Party men in suits who asked him questions for ten to twelve hours before they let him sleep. They made sure he was not comfortable and was in slight pain. They made a fool of him, made him cry.

Sometimes they said they would call the guards and their sticks again. Other times they called him 'Comrade' and asked him in the name of Big Brother to say he was sorry.

He told them he was responsible for every imaginable crime. He said he was an Eastasian spy. He said he had murdered his wife, although they knew very well she was still alive. He said he knew Goldstein . . .

He did not remember when the questions had stopped. There was a time when everything was black and then he was in this room, lying on this bed, unable to move. O'Brien was looking down at him. His hand was on a machine.

'I told you,' said O'Brien, 'that if we met again it would be here.'

'Yes,' said Winston.

O'Brien's hand touched a lever on the machine and a wave of pain passed through Winston's body.

'That was forty,' said O'Brien. 'The numbers on the dial of this machine go up to a hundred. Please remember that I can make you feel a lot of pain at any time. If you lie, if you don't answer the question or even if you answer with less than your usual intelligence, you will feel pain. Do you understand that?'

'Yes,' said Winston.

'Do you remember,' O'Brien continued, 'writing in your diary, "Freedom is the freedom to say that two and two make four"?'

'Yes,' said Winston.

O'Brien held up his left hand, its back towards Winston, with the thumb hidden and four fingers pointing forward.

'How many fingers am I holding up, Winston?'

'Four.'

'And if the Party says that it is not four but five – then how many?'

'Four.'

The word ended in a shout of pain. The dial on the machine showed fifty-five. Winston could not stop himself from crying. O'Brien touched the lever, moving it just a little, and the pain grew slightly less.

'How many fingers, Winston?'

'Four.'

O'Brien moved the lever and the dial showed sixty. 'How many fingers, Winston?'

'Four! Four! What else can I say? Four!'

The fingers swam in front of his eyes, unclear, but still four, four of them.

'How many fingers, Winston?'

'Four! Stop it, stop it! How can you continue? Four! Four!'

'How many fingers, Winston?'

'Five! Five! Five!'

'No, Winston. That's no use. You are lying. You still think there are four. How many fingers, please?'

'Four! Five! Four! Anything you like. Only stop it, stop the pain!'

Suddenly he was sitting up with O'Brien's arm round his shoulders. He felt very cold and shook uncontrollably. O'Brien held him like a baby and he felt much better. He felt that the pain was something that came from outside, and that O'Brien would save him from it.

'You are a slow learner, Winston,' said O'Brien gently.

'How can I help it?' cried Winston, through his tears. 'How

can I help seeing what is in front of my eyes? Two and two are four.'

'Sometimes, Winston. Sometimes they are five. Sometimes they are three. Sometimes they are all of them. You must try harder.'

He put Winston back down on the bed. 'Again,' he said.

The pain flamed through Winston's body. The dial was at seventy, then seventy-five. He had shut his eyes this time. He knew that the fingers were still there, and still four. He had to stay alive until the pain was over. He did not notice whether he was crying out or not. The pain grew less again. He opened his eyes.

'How many fingers, Winston?'

'Four. I would see five if I could. I am trying to see five.'

'Which do you wish: to make me believe that you see five, or really to see them?'

'Really to see them.'

'Again,' said O'Brien.

Perhaps the machine was at eighty – ninety. Winston could remember only now and again why the pain was happening. In front of his eyes a forest of fingers seemed to be moving in a kind of dance. He was trying to count them, he could not remember why. He knew only that it was impossible to count them and this was because four was in some strange way the same as five. He shut his eyes again.

'How many fingers am I holding up, Winston?'

'I don't know. I don't know. You will kill me if you do that again. Four, five, six – I honestly don't know.'

'Better,' said O'Brien.

Winston wanted to reach out his hand and touch O'Brien's arm, but he could not move. The old feeling about him came back. It did not matter if O'Brien was a friend or an enemy. O'Brien was a person he could talk to. Perhaps people did not want to be loved as much as understood. O'Brien had caused him unbelievable pain and soon would probably kill him. It made

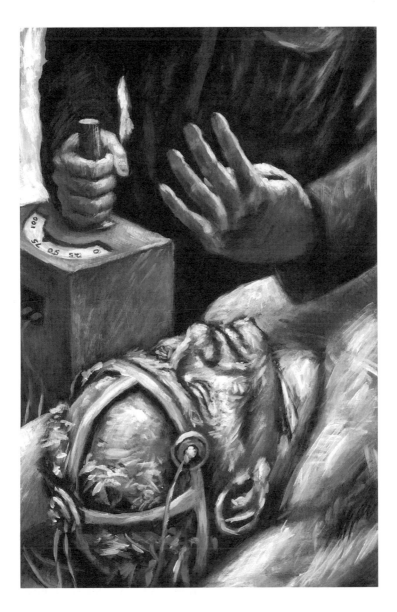

'How many fingers, Winston?'

no difference. They shared the same experiences; there was a place where they could meet and talk. O'Brien was looking down at him with a look that suggested he felt the same thing. When he spoke, it was like talking to a friend.

'Do you know where you are, Winston?' he said.

'I don't know. I can guess. In the Ministry of Love.'

'Do you know how long you have been here?'

'I don't know. Days, weeks, months – I think it is months.'

'And why do you think we bring people to this place?'

'To make them tell you about their crimes.'

'No, that is not the reason.'

'To punish them.'

'No!' shouted O'Brien. His face and voice were angry. 'No! Not just to hear about your crimes. Not just to punish you. Shall I tell you why we have brought you here? To make you better. Your crimes do not interest us. Your actions do not interest us. We are interested in your thoughts. We do not destroy our enemies, we change them. We change their thoughts. Do you understand what I mean?'

'Yes,' said Winston.

A man in a white coat came into the room and put a heavy machine behind his head. O'Brien had sat down beside the bed so he could look into Winston's eyes.

'This time it will not hurt,' said O'Brien. 'Keep looking at me.' Then he turned to the man in the white coat. 'Three thousand,' he said.

Winston felt the machine against his head. He heard a lever pulled. Then it was like an explosion inside his head, though it was not certain if there was any noise. There was blinding light and the feeling that he had been thrown back on the bed where he already was. Something had happened inside his head. As he opened his eyes he remembered who he was, and where he was, and he recognized the face that was looking down into his own;

but something was empty inside his head. It felt like a piece had been taken out of his brain.

'Look me in the eyes,' said O'Brien. He held up the four fingers of his left hand with the thumb behind the hand. 'There are five fingers there. Do you see five fingers?'

'Yes.' And he did see them, just for a second. O'Brien's words filled the hole in his mind with the complete truth.

'You see now,' said O'Brien, 'that it is possible.'

'Yes,' said Winston.

O'Brien smiled. 'I enjoy talking to you,' he said. 'Your mind is like mine, except that you are mad. Before we finish you can ask me a few questions, if you want to.'

'Any question I like?'

'Anything.' He saw that Winston's eyes were on the machine. 'It is switched off. What is your first question?'

'What have you done with Julia?' said Winston.

O'Brien smiled again. 'She betrayed you, Winston. Immediately, completely. I have never seen anybody obey us so quickly. All her feelings against the Party have been burned out of her. She has changed herself completely.'

'Did you use this machine?'

O'Brien did not answer. 'Next question,' he said.

'Does Big Brother exist?'

'Of course he exists. The Party exists. Big Brother is the face of the Party.'

'Does he exist in the same way that I exist?'

'You do not exist,' said O'Brien.

How could he not exist? But what use was it to say so? O'Brien would argue with him and win – again. 'I think I exist,' he said carefully. 'I was born and I will die. I have arms and legs. In that sense, does Big Brother exist?'

'It is not important. But, yes, Big Brother exists.'

'Will he ever die?'

'Of course not. How could he die? Next question.'

'Does the Brotherhood exist?'

'That, Winston, you will never know. If we choose to free you and if you live to be ninety years old, you will never learn whether the answer to that question is Yes or No.'

Winston lay silent. His chest moved up and down as he breathed. He still had not asked the first question that had come into his mind. He wanted to ask it but he could not move his tongue. O'Brien was smiling. He knows, thought Winston suddenly, he knows what I am going to ask. As he thought that, the words fell out of his mouth:

'What is in Room 101?'

O'Brien was still smiling. 'You know what is in Room 101, Winston. Everyone knows what is in Room 101.'


## Chapter 11  The Last Man

'There are three stages in returning you to society,' said O'Brien. 'There is learning, there is understanding and there is acceptance. It is time for you to begin the second stage.'

As always, Winston was lying flat on his back. He was still tied to the bed, but these days he was not tied so tightly. The machine, too, was less frightening. He could stop them using it if he thought quickly enough. O'Brien pulled the lever only when he said something stupid.

Winston could not remember how long this stage had lasted – weeks possibly – or how many times he had lain down on the bed, talking to O'Brien.

'You have read *the book*, Goldstein's book, or parts of it,' said O'Brien. 'Did it tell you anything that you did not know already?'

'You have read it?' said Winston.

'I wrote it. I was *one* of the people who wrote it. No book is written by one person, as you know.'

'Is any of it true?'

'It describes our situation truthfully, yes. Its solutions make no sense at all. The *proles* will never attack the Party or even criticize it. Not in a thousand years or a million. They cannot. I do not have to tell you the reason: you know it already. The Party will rule for all time. Make that the starting point of your thoughts. Now, let us turn to the question of *why* we are ruling. What do you think?'

Winston said what he thought O'Brien wanted to hear. 'You are ruling over us for our own good,' he said. 'You believe that people are not able to govern themselves and so . . .'

He screamed. Pain had shot through his body. The machine showed thirty-five.

'That was stupid, Winston, stupid!' said O'Brien. 'You should know better than to say a thing like that.' He switched the machine off and continued. 'Now I will tell you the answer to my question. The Party is only interested in power – not in the happiness of others, or money, or long life. We want power, only power, pure power. And we will never, never let it go. Now do you begin to understand me?'

Winston thought how tired O'Brien looked. O'Brien moved forward in his chair, bringing his face close to Winston's.

'You are thinking,' he said, 'that my face is old and tired. You are thinking that I talk of power but I cannot stop my own body getting old. Can you not understand, Winston, that each person is only a very small part of something much bigger? And when the small part needs changing, the whole grows stronger. Do you die when you cut your hair?'

O'Brien turned away from the bed and began to walk up and down. 'You must understand that power belongs to the group, not to one person. An individual has power only when he belongs to a group so completely that he is not an individual any more. The Party says that "Freedom is Slavery" but the opposite is also true. Slavery is Freedom. Alone – free – a human being will die in the end. But if he can be completely part of the Party, not an individual, then he can do anything and he lives for all time. The second thing is that power means power over the human body but, above all, power over the human mind. We already control everything else.'

For a moment Winston forgot about the machine. 'How can you say that you control everything? You can't control the weather. You don't even control the Earth. What about Eurasia and Eastasia? You don't control them.'

'Unimportant. We shall control them when we want to. And if we did not, what difference would it make? Oceania is the world. Have you forgotten *doublethink*?'

Winston lay back on the bed. He knew he was right. O'Brien was saying that nothing exists outside your own mind. There must be a way of showing this was wrong?

O'Brien was smiling. 'The real power,' he said, 'is not power over things, but over men.' He paused and for a moment looked like a teacher talking to a clever schoolboy. 'How does one man show that he has power over another man, Winston?'

Winston thought. 'By making him suffer,' he said.

'Exactly. By making him suffer. Power means causing pain. Power lies in taking human minds to pieces and putting them together again in new shapes of your own choice. Do you begin to see, then, what kind of world we are making? It is the opposite of the stupid worlds which people used to imagine, worlds of love and pleasure. We have built a world of fear and suffering and hate. We shall destroy everything else – everything. We are destroying the love between child and parent, between man and man, and between man and woman. In the future there will be no wives and no friends. Children will be taken from their mothers when they are born. There will be no love, except the love of Big Brother. Nobody will laugh, except at an enemy they have destroyed. There will be no art, no literature, no science. If you want a picture of the future, Winston, imagine a boot stamping on a human face – for ever.'

Winston could not say anything. His heart seemed frozen.

O'Brien continued: 'You are beginning, I can see, to understand what that world will be like. But in the end you will do more than understand it. You will accept it, welcome it, become part of it.'

Winston was still just strong enough to speak. 'You can't,' he said weakly.

'What do you mean, Winston?'

'If a society were built on hate, it would fall to pieces.'

'No, no. You think that hating is more tiring than loving. Why should it be? And even if it was true, what difference would it make?'

Winston was helpless again, unable to argue, unable to find the words to explain the horror that he felt. 'Something will beat you,' he said, finally. 'Life will beat you.'

'We control life, Winston. And we control the way people are. People can be changed very easily, you know.'

'No! I know that you will fail. There is something in all human beings that will beat you.'

'And are you a human being, Winston? Are you a man?'

'Yes.'

'If you are a man, Winston, you are the last man. Your kind of man is finished. Do you understand that you are *alone*? You are outside history, you do not exist.' His voice changed as he gave Winston a hard look. 'And you think you are better than us, because we hate and cause pain?'

'Yes, I think I am better.'

O'Brien did not speak. Two other voices were speaking. After a moment Winston recognized one of the voices as his own. It was the conversation he had had with O'Brien on the night he had joined the Brotherhood. He heard himself promising to murder another person, to cause the death of hundreds of innocent people, to make a child blind and destroy its face. O'Brien pressed a switch and the voices stopped.

'Get up from the bed,' he said.

Winston got off the bed and stood up with difficulty.

'You are the last man,' said O'Brien. 'Are you really better than us? You're going to see yourself as you are. Take off your clothes.'

Winston took his dirty overalls off and saw himself in a three-sided mirror at the end of the room. He cried out at the horrible sight.

'Move closer,' said O'Brien. 'Look at yourself closely in the three mirrors.'

Winston had stopped walking towards the mirror because he was frightened. A bent, grey-coloured thing was walking towards him in the mirror. His face was completely changed. He had very little hair, his back was bent, he was terribly thin. This looked like the body of an old, dying man.

'You have thought sometimes,' said O'Brien, 'that my face – the face of a member of the Inner Party – looks old and tired. What do you think of your own face?' He pulled out a handful of Winston's hair. 'Even your hair is coming out in handfuls. Open your mouth. Nine, ten, eleven teeth left. How many did you have when you came to us? And they are dropping out of your head. Look here!'

He took hold of one of Winston's few front teeth between his thumb and two fingers. Pain filled Winston's face. O'Brien had pulled out the loose tooth. He threw it across the cell.

'You are falling to pieces,' he said. 'You are dirty. Did you know you smell like a dog? What are you? Just a dirty animal. Now look into that mirror again. That is the last man.'

Before he knew what he was doing, Winston had sat on a small chair near the mirror and started to cry. 'You did it!' he said, through his tears. 'You made me look like this.'

O'Brien put a hand on his shoulder, almost kindly. 'No, Winston. You did it yourself when you stopped obeying the Party.' He paused for a moment and then continued. 'We have beaten you, Winston. We have broken you. You have seen your body. Your mind is in the same state. There is nothing that we did not make you do.'

Winston stopped crying. 'I have not betrayed Julia,' he said.

O'Brien looked down at him thoughtfully. 'No,' he said. 'No, that is true. You have not betrayed Julia.'

Winston thought again how intelligent O'Brien was. Nothing, it seemed, could stop him admiring the man. O'Brien had understood that Winston still loved Julia and that meant more than betraying the details of their meetings.

'Tell me,' he said. 'How soon will they shoot me?'

'It might be a long time,' said O'Brien. 'You are a difficult case. But don't give up hope. Everyone is cured sooner or later. In the end we shall shoot you.'

## Chapter 12 Room 101

He was much better. He was getting fatter and stronger every day. The new cell was more comfortable than the others he had been in. There was a bed and a chair to sit on. There was paper and an ink-pencil. They had given him a bath and they let him wash frequently in a metal bowl. They even gave him warm water to wash with. They had given him new overalls, pulled out the rest of his teeth and given him new false teeth.

Weeks had passed, perhaps months. He could count time passing by his meals; he received, he thought, three meals in twenty-four hours. The food was surprisingly good, with meat every third meal. Once there was even a packet of cigarettes.

His mind grew more active. He sat down on his bed, his back against the wall, and began to re-train his mind. He belonged to them now, that was agreed. As he realized now, he had given in, he had been ready to belong to them, a long time before he had made the decision. From his first moment inside the Ministry of Love – and yes, even when he and Julia stood helpless in front of the *telescreen* in Charrington's room – he had understood that it had been stupid to fight against the power of the Party.

He knew that for seven years the Thought Police had watched him, looking down on him like an insect walking along a path. They knew everything that he had said or done. They had played his voice back to him, shown him photographs. Some of them were photographs of Julia and himself. Yes, even . . . He could not fight against the Party now. And why should he? The Party was right.

He began to write, with big child-like letters:

FREEDOM IS SLAVERY

TWO AND TWO MAKE FIVE

And while he worked on *crimestop* inside his mind, he wondered when they would shoot him. They might keep him here for years, they might let him out for a short time – as they sometimes did. But one day they would shoot him. You never knew when. Often they shot you from behind, in the back of the head.

One day – or one night perhaps – he had a dream. He was waiting for them to shoot him. He was out in the sunshine and he called out, 'Julia! Julia! My love! Julia!'

He lay back on the bed, frightened. How many years had he added to his time in this cell by shouting out her name?

There was the noise of boots outside. O'Brien walked into the cell. Behind him were the officer with the emotionless face and the black-uniformed guards.

'You have had thoughts of betraying me,' he said. 'That was stupid. Tell me, Winston – and tell me the truth because I will know if you are lying – tell me, what do you really think of Big Brother?'

'I hate him.'

'You hate him. Good. Then the time has come for you to take the last step. You must love Big Brother.'

He pushed Winston towards the guards. 'Room 101,' he said.

◆

Winston always knew if the cells were high up or low down in the building. The air was different. This place was many metres underground, as deep down as it was possible to go.

It was bigger than most of the cells he had been in. There were two small tables in front of him. One was a metre or two away, the other was near the door. He was tied to a chair so tightly that he could not move, not even his head. He had to look straight in front of him.

O'Brien came in. 'You asked me once,' he said, 'what was in Room 101. I said that you knew the answer already. Everyone knows it. In Room 101 there is the worst thing in the world.'

The door opened again. A guard came in carrying a box. There was a tube at the front of it. He put it down on the table near the door.

'The worst thing in the world,' said O'Brien, 'is different for each person. It may be death by fire, or by water, or fifty other deaths. Sometimes it is something quite small, that does not even kill you.'

He had moved to one side and Winston could now see what was on the table. It was a big metal box and through holes in the sides he could see movement. Rats.

'For you,' said O'Brien, 'the worst thing in the world is rats.'

Winston had been afraid before, but suddenly he understood what the tube was for. He felt very, very sick.

'You can't do that!' he screamed. 'O'Brien! What do you want me to do?'

'Pain alone,' said O'Brien quietly, 'is not always enough. The rat,' he continued, like a teacher giving a lesson, 'eats meat. In the poor parts of the town a mother cannot leave her baby outside because in ten minutes there will only be bones left. Rats are also very intelligent. They know when a human being is helpless.'

The rats were big and brown, they were making little high cries, fighting with each other. O'Brien moved the box until it was a metre from Winston's face.

'You understand this box and tube? One end of the tube goes into the box and the other, wider end goes over your face. When I press this switch, a door into the tube will open and the rats will run along it towards your face. Sometimes they attack the eyes first. Sometimes they eat through the face, into the tongue.'

One end of the tube was put over his face. He could see the first rat, its face, its teeth.

He knew there was only one hope, one last hope. He needed to put someone else between himself and that rat. He needed to give them someone else. And he heard himself shouting, screaming, 'Do it to Julia! Do it to Julia! Not me! Julia! I don't care what you do to her. Destroy her face, leave only bones. Not me! Julia! Not me!'

He heard O'Brien touch the switch and knew he had closed the door to the tube, not opened it.

◆

The Chestnut Tree Café was almost empty. It was the lonely time of fifteen hours. Music came from the *telescreens* now but Winston was listening for news of the war. Oceania was at war with Eurasia. Oceania had always been at war with Eurasia. He drank a glass of gin, although it tasted terrible. A waiter brought him that day's *Times*.

His finger moved on the table. He wrote in the dust:

$2 + 2 = 5$

'They can't get inside you,' she had said. But they *could* get inside you. And when they did, something inside you died.

*He wrote in the dust:*
*2 + 2 = 5*

He had seen her; he had even spoken to her. There was no danger in it. He knew that. They took no interest in him now. They could even see each other again if either of them wanted to. But they did not want to.

He had met her by chance in the park on a cold day in March. She was fatter now. She had walked away from him at first. When he caught her, he put his arm round her waist but did not try to kiss her. He did not want to kiss her.

They sat down on two iron chairs, not too close together. There were no *telescreens* here but possibly hidden microphones. It did not matter.

'I betrayed you,' she said.

'I betrayed you, too,' he said.

'In the end they do something so terrible that you say "Don't do it to me, do it to somebody else, do it to the person I love." You only care about yourself.'

'You only care about yourself,' he had agreed.

And he had meant it. He had not just said it, he had wished it. He had wanted her at the end of the tube when they . . .

Something changed on the *telescreen* in the Chestnut Tree Café. The music stopped and the face of Big Brother filled the *telescreen*. Winston looked up at the enormous face with the moustache. Tears ran down his face and he was happy. He had won the fight with himself. He loved Big Brother.

# ACTIVITIES

## Chapters 1–2

*Before you read*

1 In *1984*, George Orwell warns us how future governments could make life worse for ordinary people. How might future governments use these to make life worse?

   computers   schools   cameras   information

2 Look at the Word List at the back of the book. Find words for:
   a groups or organizations of people
   b people
   c places where people spend time
   d actions through which other people could harm you
   e things that you can buy in a shop

*While you read*

3 Are these sentences about Winston true (✓) or false (✗)?
   a He is a big man with dark hair.                          .....
   b He turns off the *telescreen*.                           .....
   c He works in the Ministry of Truth.                       .....
   d He joins the Two Minutes Hate.                           .....
   e He throws a dictionary at the *telescreen*.              .....
   f He breaks the law.                                       .....
   g He organizes evening activities for the Party.           .....
   h He is hurt by a bomb.                                    .....

*After you read*

4 Who or what are these? How are they important to Big Brother?
   *telescreens*
   *Miniluv*
   Emmanuel Goldstein
   the Thought Police
   Newspeak

**5** How does Winston feel about these? Why?

    **a** his childhood

    **b** *telescreens*

    **c** the Thought Police

    **d** the girl from the Fiction Department

    **e** Emmanuel Goldstein

    **f** O'Brien

    **g** his diary

**6** Discuss these questions with another student. What do you think?

    **a** Look at the slogans on page 2. Can you think of any more slogans for Big Brother?

    **b** What happens inside the Ministry of Love?

    **c** Why is Oceania always at war?

    **d** What is Winston really thinking while he is shouting at the *telescreen*?

    **e** Are Winston and Tom Parsons friends? Why (not)?

## Chapters 3–4

*Before you read*

**7** Discuss these questions.

    **a** What do you think these Newspeak words might mean?

       *speakwrite  unperson  ungood  facecrime  ownlife*

    **b** What do you think workers do at the Ministry of Truth?

*While you read*

**8** Who or what are these sentences about?

    **a** Winston re-writes part of it. ........................

    **b** It does not exist in the Ministry of Truth. ........................

    **c** He is a hero who never existed. ........................

    **d** Ampleforth re-writes them. ........................

    **e** Syme is re-writing it. ........................

**f** It brings tears to Winston's eyes. ........................

**g** Winston talks to them in the
canteen. ........................

**h** They were *vaporized* in the 1950s. ........................

**i** Party members do not usually go
there. ........................

**j** Winston bought it from Charrington. ........................

*After you read*

**9** Look at your answers to question 7a. Were your answers correct?
If not, what are the right answers?

**10** Answer these questions.

Why:

**a** does Winston think that Syme will be *vaporized*?

**b** does Winston look with disbelief at the *telescreen* in the
canteen?

**c** did Winston and his wife separate?

What:

**d** is the largest department in the Ministry of Truth?

**e** happens in the underground rooms below the Ministry of
Love?

**f** does Winston like about the small room above Charrington's
shop?

**11** Work with another student. Have this conversation between
Winston and a member of the Thought Police.

Student A: You are the Thought Police Officer. You think that
Winston is guilty of *thoughtcrime*, *facecrime* and
*ownlife*. Tell him why.

Student B: You are Winston. Tell the Thought Police Officer why
you are not guilty of the crimes. Make your lies as
believable as possible!

## Chapters 5–6

*Before you read*

**12** Look at the pictures in Chapters 5 and 6. Who is the girl in these pictures? What do you already know about her? How do you think she will be important in the next part of the story?

*While you read*

**13** Circle the correct words.

    **a** Winston reads the girl's message in *his office / the toilet*.

    **b** The countryside is a *dangerous / safe* place to meet.

    **c** Julia is *much / slightly* younger than Winston.

    **d** Julia likes Winston because he *hates the Party / is good-looking*.

    **e** Winston *is / is not* Julia's first boyfriend.

    **f** Julia likes *books / machinery*.

    **g** Katherine did not tell the Thought Police about her husband because she was *afraid / unintelligent*.

    **h** Winston thinks that he and Julia *will / will not* be caught.

*After you read*

**14** Who is speaking? Who to? What do the underlined words mean?

    **a** 'Can you remember all <u>that</u>?'

    **b** 'I hated the sight of <u>you</u>.'

    **c** '<u>It</u>'s the only way to be safe.'

    **d** 'When I first saw you, I knew you were against <u>them</u>.'

    **e** 'Have you done <u>this</u> before?'

    **f** '<u>This</u> is the one I'm really proud of.'

    **g** '<u>It</u>'s the one thing <u>they</u> can't do.'

    **h** '<u>They</u> are the most horrible things in the world.'

**15** Discuss these questions with another student. What do you think? Why?

    **a** Do Julia and Winston really love each other?

    **b** How does Winston feel about Julia's other boyfriends? Do you agree with him?

    **c** Is Winston right to rent the room above Mr Charrington's shop?

**Chapters 7–8**

*Before you read*

**16** Read again the last sentence in Chapter 6 and discuss these questions with another student:

    **a** In what sense is the room 'a world'?

    **b** In what sense is it a 'past world'?

    **c** In what sense are Winston and Julia the last two people who are still living?

    **d** What do you think the future will be like for them?

*While you read*

**17** In which order do these happen? Number them 1–8.

    **a** Winston thinks about the importance of the *proles*.   .....

    **b** Winston and Julia drink to Emmanuel Goldstein.   .....

    **c** Winston reads Goldstein's book.   .....

    **d** Syme disappears.   .....

    **e** Oceania goes to war with Eastasia.   .....

    **f** Winston tells Julia about O'Brien.   .....

    **g** Soldiers come into Mr Charrington's shop.   .....

    **h** Winstone and Julia visit O'Brien.   .....

*After you read*

**18** Match the correct endings on page 74 for these sentences.

    **a** Parsons is happy because he …   .....

    **b** Julia disagrees with Winston because she …   .....

    **c** Winston feels sure that O'Brien is against the Party because O'Brien …   .....

    **d** Winston and Julia re surprised because O'Brien …   .....

    **e** Winston tells O'Brien his secret because he …   .....

    **f** Winston cannot taste the wine because he …   .....

    **g** At the beginning of the twentieth century, equality became possible because machines …   .....

    **h** The Middle and Low groups could not move up in society because the Inner Party …   .....

**i** The Party is never criticized because nobody ... .....

**j** Winston is shocked because Mr Charrington ... .....

**1)** usually drinks gin.

**2)** can remember the past.

**3)** did most of the work.

**4)** can switch off the *telescreen*.

**5)** owned almost everything.

**6)** is helping to organize Hate Week.

**7)** talks about an *unperson*.

**8)** thinks that Goldstein does not exist.

**9)** is a member of the Thought Police.

**10)** wants to join the Brotherhood.

**19** Is the Party for or against these things? Why?

equality *doublethink* war history the Brotherhood

## Chapters 9–10

*Before you read*

**20** How do you think these might be important in the next part of the story?

The Ministry of Love O'Brien Ampleforth Parsons pain Winston's diary

*While you read*

**21** Underline the correct answer.

**a** Ampleforth is a prisoner because he

**1)** is guilty of *thoughtcrime*.

**2)** uses a wrong word in a poem.

**b** Parsons feels

**1)** proud of his daughter.

**2)** angry with Big Brother.

**c** Winston suffers great pain because he does not believe

**1)** what he is told.

**2)** that he is guilty.

**d** O'Brien wants to
**1)** change Winston.
**2)** punish Winston.
**e** O'Brien refuses to tell Winston
**1)** what happened to Julia.
**2)** whether the Brotherhood exists.

*After you read*

**22** Discuss these questions with another student.

    **a** Who does Winston think about most when he first arrives at the Ministry of Love? Why?

    **b** O'Brien says 'You knew this, Winston. You have always known it.' What is he talking about?

    **c** Why is O'Brien so interested in the number of fingers he shows Winston?

    **d** Does Winston hate O'Brien? Why (not)?

**Chapters 11–12**

*Before you read*

**23** Discuss these questions.

    **a** What do you think is going to happen to Winston in Room 101?

    **b** Will there be a happy ending for Winston and Julia? Why (not)?

*While you read*

**24** There is one wrong word in each sentence. Underline it and write the correct word.

    **a** O'Brien wrote all of Goldstein's book. ........................

    **b** The Party is not interested in power, long life or happiness. ........................

    **c** O'Brien thinks that the individual is more important than the group. ........................

    **d** In the future, there will be no art, literature or music. ........................

    **e** O'Brien shows Winston a picture. ........................

**f** Room 101 is the second stage in
Winston's return to society. ........................

**g** O'Brien opens the door to the tube
because Winston has betrayed Julia. ........................

**h** When Winston sees Big Brother on the
*telescreen* in the Chestnut Tree Café,
he feels sad. ........................

*After you read*

**25** Do you agree with these opinions of *1984*? Why (not)? Discuss
your ideas with another student.

**a** The book is still popular because it is a great love story and a
great adventure story.

**b** The world of *1984* will never come true.

**c** The world of *1984* has already come true.

**d** The story would be better if it had a happier ending.

## Writing

**26** Imagine that you are Syme (Chapter 3). Invent ten new words for
the Newspeak dictionary. What do they mean?

**27** Imagine that you are Winston at the end of Chapter 4. Write about
recent events in your diary. Describe the people that you know
and your feelings about them.

**28** Imagine that you are a Party spy. Write a report on the activities of
Winston and Julia in Chapters 5 and 6.

**29** What happened to Syme (Chapter 7)? Why was he *vaporized*?
Write his story.

**30** Imagine that you are Julia (Chapter 6). Write a letter to a friend
about Winston. What is he like? Why do you like him? What are
your plans together?

**31** Write a list of Party rules for people in Oceania. What are they not
allowed to do, according to the story?

**32** Write a short history of Oceania from 1950–1984, according to
Goldstein's book (Chapter 8).

**33** 'The future belonged to the *proles*; Party members were the dead.' (Chapter 8) Imagine you are Winston. Explain your ideas in an article for a political magazine against the Party.

**34** O'Brien says, 'The worst thing in the world is different for each person.' (Chapter 12) What would be in *your* Room 101? Why?

**35** Imagine that you are Julia (Chapter 12). Write a letter to Winston. Describe your experiences in the Ministry of Love. Why can't you see him again?

Answers for the Activities in this book are available from the Penguin Readers website. A free Activity Worksheet is also available from the website. Activity Worksheets are part of the Penguin Teacher Support Programme, which also includes Progress Tests and Graded Reader Guidelines. For more information, please visit: www.penguinreaders.com.

# WORD LIST

**article** (n) a piece of writing in a newspaper or magazine

**betray** (v) to harm a person, group or country by telling their secrets

**brotherhood** (n) an organization of people with the same aims or beliefs

**canteen** (n) a place in an office, factory or school where people go to eat and drink

**cell** (n) a small room where prisoners are kept

**comrade** (n) a word used to talk to or about a person in some socialist groups or countries

**dial** (n) the part of a machine that has numbers which show you measurements

**edition** (n) the copies of a book, newspaper or magazine that are all the same

**freedom** (n) the state of being free to live your life as you want to

**gin** (n) a clear, strong alcoholic drink

**hang** (v) to kill someone by tying something around their neck and taking the support away from under their feet

**ignorance** (n) the state of having no knowledge or information about something

**individual** (n) one person in a group or society

**league** (n) a group of people with similar aims or beliefs

**lever** (n) a handle on a machine that you push to make the machine work

**mansions** (n pl) a word used in the name for a building in which there are a lot of flats

**ministry** (n) a government department

**overalls** (n pl) a piece of clothing that you wear over your shirt and trousers to protect them

**party** (n) an organization of people with the same political aims

**poster** (n) a large notice or picture

**prole** (n) a working-class person (often an offensive word when used now)

**razor blade** (n) the small, sharp, flat piece of metal inside a razor that is used for shaving